Seoulmates

Seoulmates
Korea Through Indian Eyes

Sudha Huzurbazar Tumbe and
Vasudev Tumbe

JUGGERNAUT BOOKS
C-I-128, First Floor, Sangam Vihar, Near Holi Chowk,
New Delhi 110080, India

First published by Juggernaut Books 2025

Copyright © Sudha Huzurbazar Tumbe and Vasudev Tumbe 2025

10 9 8 7 6 5 4 3 2 1

P-ISBN: 9789353454111
E-ISBN: 9789353457044

The views and opinions expressed in this book are the authors' own. The facts contained herein were reported to be true as on the date of publication by the authors to the publishers of the book, and the publishers are not in any way liable for their accuracy or veracity.

All rights reserved. No part of this publication may be reproduced, transmitted, or stored in a retrieval system in any form or by any means without the written permission of the publisher.

Typeset in Adobe Caslon Pro by Mukul Chand

Printed at Replika Press Pvt. Ltd.

Dedicated to

*Our parents,
who shaped us,
and
our son Chinmay,
daughter-in-law Divya
and grandson Siddhartha,
for motivating us to write!*

Contents

	Prologue	ix
1.	Land of Morning Calm	1
2.	Miracle on the Han River	19
3.	'Uri Nara' Mantra	63
4.	Work–Life Imbalance?	109
5.	Life Without a Work Visa	157
6.	Travel in Four Seasons	201
	Afterword	221
	Acknowledgements	231
	A Note on the Authors	233
	Glossary of Korean Words in the Book	235

Prologue

When Sudha's book *Saptarangi Korea: Ek Anubhav* was published in Marathi by Granthali in December 2022, many people asked her, 'Why not in English?' Sudha was quick to respond, 'Vasudev will do that.'

Having worked in finance and accounts all my life, I have been a 'numbers' guy and generally a man of few words. 'At best,' I said, 'I can write a one-page executive summary. But a book? No way!'

After seeing the positive response to Sudha's Marathi book and the growing interest about South Korea in India, especially among Gen Z – thanks to Korean dramas and K-pop – I thought it would be worthwhile to document our experiences in Korea. I felt this could be useful to an Indian reader who wants to know more about South Korea from an Indian perspective.

Sudha's book had a theme. It was based on the seven colours of the rainbow, each colour highlighting some Korean characteristic seen through an Indian prism. It was not possible to translate the same into English, as the order of rainbow colours in English is different and the essence would have been lost.

This book includes Sudha's experiences, to which I have added my own corporate life experience in Korea, a brief history of the country, how it managed to become a developed country within two generations and what learnings Indians can glean from Korea's economic miracle story. The K-wave part in Chapter 2, and Chapters 5 and 6 are written in Sudha's voice, and the rest of the book is in my voice.

The book is about South Korea, where we had the privilege to live for over six years, from 2013 to 2019. In this book, we have used 'Korea' to mean South Korea most of the time, unless the context speaks of a time before its division. 'North Korea' is mentioned only where we refer to that geopolitical entity and at times, 'South Korea' is mentioned for clarity or emphasis.

Full Korean names have been used for real people and only Korean surnames have been used if a person's identity was not to be disclosed.

I would like to add a caveat here. This book is about our experiences in Korea, which were very enjoyable and memorable. The same may not be true for everyone else. I was fortunate to have a comfortable life with an English-speaking driver and an interpreter in office. Sudha was able to enjoy her time in the country because she learnt the language, and went out of her way to make new friends and try different cuisines. The experiences may have been different if we were strict vegetarians or students, or were just starting our careers.

The biggest lessons we learnt were to appreciate the culture of a new country, assimilate with its people and be ambassadors of our own country because, no matter where one goes in the world, we always represent the country we come from.

– Vasudev Tumbe

I love to travel and make new friends. The first time Korea caught my attention was during the 1988 Seoul Olympics. Soon after, however, our focus shifted to Japan, what with its then-ubiquitous products and brands like Sony TV, National VCR, Hitachi music player and Maruti Suzuki car. So much so that I started learning Japanese in 1990. At the time, our travels were restricted to India with an occasional foreign trip thrown in.

The twenty-first century heralded a change in our personal lifestyle and a greater use of Korean products when Hyundai, Samsung and LG became household names in India. We started going for annual foreign trips but Korea was still not on our radar. There were many other countries on our bucket list and Korea could wait.

In December 2012, I celebrated my fiftieth birthday in Mumbai in the presence of family and friends. This was a time in our lives when Vasudev would be busy with office work throughout the week, and I with my various interests. I would spend three days every week at Lotus Eye Hospital, Juhu, as a low vision rehabilitation specialist; two days at Veermata Jijabai Technological Institute

(VJTI) Engineering College, teaching management as a guest faculty to final year engineering students; and on Saturday and Sunday, I would teach a distance education programme at Shreemati Nathibai Damodar Thackersey (SNDT) Women's University, Juhu.

All this was to change when Vasudev told me in late December 2012 that he had been offered a position as the CFO of SsangYong Motor Company based out of Korea and that he had accepted it. I was surprised to hear this news but was not unhappy that he had already accepted the position without discussing it with me. This is because we had already spoken about it in the past, that if any international assignment came our way, we should take up the challenge and use it as a way to expand our horizons.

Vasudev's transfer was yet to be confirmed by the Korean CEO of SsangYong, and we were supposed to go to Korea for a 'look and see'. We arrived there in March 2013 with the assumption that we may not be transferred after all, so we decided to make the most of the opportunity to see Seoul. When Vasudev was busy with work, I went sightseeing using the efficient public transport, especially the metro. Occasionally, when Vasudev was free, we went around in his company car.

My first impression of Korea was love at first sight. The beautiful airport, the wide roads, the cleanliness and the friendly people who did not seem to mind that I did not know their language made me want to stay on. I said to myself, 'Now, it does not matter whether Vasudev gets a transfer or not, I have seen the place. But I hope we get transferred to Korea. I want to live more in this country.'

As it turned out, Vasudev did get the transfer, and we started packing to move to Seoul in July 2013. It felt like I was going to start life afresh at 50!

When we bid goodbye to our friends in Mumbai, many were surprised and asked us questions like, 'Does your son live in Korea?', 'Why are you going abroad at this age, that too to an unknown country?', 'Are you going to North or South Korea? We read reports of some conflict between North and South.'

We reached Seoul on 6 July 2013 on a direct Korean Air flight from Mumbai. After a nine-hour journey that was quite comfortable, we were welcomed at the Incheon Airport by our driver, Jay, who was holding a placard that said, 'Welcome Mr Tumbe, SsangYong Motor Company.'

With our six bags, we entered 301-I Park, 1604, our new home for the next 36 months, which eventually turned into home for the next six years and six months.

– Sudha Huzurbazar Tumbe

1
Land of Morning Calm

When I joined SsangYong Motor Company in July 2013 and was going through my appointment calendar for August, I asked my interpreter Ms Park, 'Why do we have a holiday on 15 August?'

'It's Independence Day,' she replied.

'Is it because this company is owned by an Indian company (the Mahindra group) that we have a holiday to celebrate India's independence?' I asked.

'No, it is Korea's Independence Day!' she said in a surprised tone.

Now it was my turn to be surprised. I had just come to a new country and had done some reading about Korea, especially the business aspect, yet was totally ignorant of this fact. I assumed 15 August meant only one thing – India's Independence Day.

After recovering from my surprise, I asked Ms Park, 'Independence from whom?'

'From Japan. We were a colony of Japan's from 1910 to 1945 and got independence after World War II, on 15 August 1945.'

'What a coincidence! India got independence from British colonial rule on 15 August 1947,' I exclaimed.

'Indeed, a coincidence!' Ms Park agreed.

As we will see by the end of this chapter, this was not really a coincidence.

I resumed my work and decided that I must learn more about Korea's history before any other embarrassing incidents occurred.

To be honest, before going to Seoul in 2013, I did not know anything about the country except that it was a leader in manufacturing electronics and automobiles – I had been using Korean household products made by the likes of Samsung, LG and Hyundai.

Brief History

I started reading and discussing Korean history with my Korean friends. Korea was ruled by the Silla dynasty from the seventh to the mid-tenth century, then by the Goryeo dynasty from the tenth to the end of the fourteenth century. Modern Korea got its name from this dynasty's name, 'Goryeo'. The Joseon dynasty that followed ruled for five centuries, from the end of the fourteenth century to the end of the nineteenth century.

Towards the end of the nineteenth century, Japan was developing rapidly and getting ambitious. When it won the war against China in 1895, Japan became a dominant force and attempted to gain control of Korea to have a strategic foothold in the region. In 1910, it annexed Korea, deposing the Joseon king. From 1910 to 1945, Korea was a colony of Japan. The Japanese modernized some of the infrastructure and education systems, but their aggressive approach in imposing their language and customs, and their exploitation of labour was resented by the Koreans – the undercurrents of which are felt even today. At the end of World War II, Japan was defeated, and this resulted in Korea's freedom.

At this time, Korea was divided along the 38th parallel into Soviet-occupied North Korea and US-occupied South Korea. After the attempts to form one united country failed, in 1948, two separate states were established: Republic of Korea (South) backed by the US and Democratic People's Republic of Korea (DPRK; North) with the support of the USSR. From 1948 to 1950, there was constant turmoil and conflict on both sides of the 38th parallel.

In June 1950, North Korean forces invaded South Korea and captured Seoul. A United Nations (UN) force led by the US intervened and pushed the North Korean forces back across the 38th parallel. When the UN forces went deeper into North Korea, close to the Chinese border, China entered the fray. The war escalated and continued for three years, with heavy casualties and destruction of property on both sides.

The three-year-long Korean War reached a stalemate and an armistice was signed in July 1953, establishing the Korean Demilitarized Zone (DMZ) near the 38th parallel. The DMZ continues to serve as a buffer between the two countries till today, well-guarded by soldiers on both sides.

A peace treaty was never signed and the Korean peninsula remains divided.

Many of our guests from India would be keen to see the DMZ, which was 75 km from our place. An interesting part of the DMZ tour was the tunnels that were dug by the North Koreans to secretly come south to attack South Korea. The tunnels were discovered (before any attack could be launched) in the 1970s and have become a tourist attraction today. There is a railway station at the DMZ that technically is the last stop, but it is heartening to note that this is called the first station (to North Korea), symbolizing a ray of hope that reunification will happen someday.

Ironically, North Korea, ruled by a dictator, is called Democratic People's Republic of Korea. The US maintains a military presence in South Korea to guard it against a possible North Korean attack. Currently, there are more than 25,000 US military personnel stationed there. North Korea continues to be a threat in the region, with its ambitious nuclear plans and frequent testing of missiles.

The end of World War II had brought about divisions in Korea and Germany under similar circumstances (under the influence of the communist Soviet Union versus the capitalist US). While West and East Germany have since united, it is unfortunate that Korea continues to remain divided even after more than 70 years.

When I spoke to my South Korean friends on the subject of possible unification in the future, I did not get any hostility or angst, only concern. While speaking to elderly people, I heard a mixed response. Some have a soft corner for the North, having seen the effects of separation or experienced them through relatives and friends. After all, they were one country once with the same language, food habits and culture. Some have bitter experiences and are apprehensive about any talks of peace after having witnessed several aggressive moves from the North. As for the younger generations, they seemed to be more open to the possibilities of dialogue and peace, though concerned about the economic impact.

Politically, some groups lean towards a more hard-line approach, whereas some prefer the route of dialogue and engagement to foster peaceful relations. While everybody hopes that there will be no escalation or war between the two countries, the major concern among the people I spoke to was the huge economic impact the South will have to bear in the event of a reunification. Some see it as an opportunity for economic growth through the development of new markets and availability of greater resources. However, with the wide gap in the economic status of the two countries, it is clear that South Koreans will have to sacrifice much more to integrate with the North, whenever or if it ever happens. Nobody seems to be in a hurry for reunification, and I got a feeling from my friends that if it has to happen, it should happen gradually.

Geography and Demography

Korea is situated in northeast Asia, between Japan and China. From its capital city Seoul, it is a two-hour flight to Tokyo as well as to Beijing, and only 70 km to the North Korean border.

South Korea is a relatively small country of about 100,000 sq. km (almost one-third the size of an Indian state like Maharashtra) with a population of a little over 51 million people.

Christianity (more Protestant than Catholic) and Buddhism are the major religions, but the majority do not practise any religion. Almost all the people worship their ancestors during the Lunar New Year (Seollal) and Harvest Festival (Chuseok).

Like Japan, Korea too has an aged population, with an average life expectancy of 82 years.

Indian Princess Connection

Before coming to the present, let me take a step back into Korea's history to about 2,000 years ago. It so happened, one day in 2017, a close Indian friend in Seoul was so impressed by the safety and governance in Korea that he likened it to 'Ramrajya', which, according to Hindu mythology, refers to 'Lord Rama's governance', under which people felt safe and happy. I felt this was too exaggerated but did not want to disagree. Thus, what followed came as a great surprise – a link to Lord Rama's birthplace, Ayodhya.

Our friend told us that Koreans believe that their connection with India goes back 2,000 years. As per *Samguk Yusa*, a thirteenth-century collection of legends and historical accounts, a princess named Suriratna from Ayodhya undertook a long sea voyage to Korea with her brother in 48 AD to marry the Korean king Kim Su-ro, and eventually came to be known as Queen Heo Hwang-ok. As legend goes, Suriratna's father had had a dream that he must send his daughter across the seas, while King Kim Su-ro had also had a dream that his bride would come from a faraway land. Some researchers point out that *Samyuk Yusa* mentioned the place from where Suriratna had come as 'Ayuta', which many interpret to be the Indian city of Ayodhya. King Kim Su-ro and Queen Heo Hwang-ok had 12 children, and it is said that today almost 10 per cent of Korea's population are descendants of this couple. In present-day Gimhae city, in Southeast Korea, there is a tomb that is said to be of Queen Heo Hwang-ok, which our friend happened to visit.

A year later, we decided to find out more about this from our friends at the Indian embassy, and what we got to know was again a revelation. While India and Korea have had diplomatic ties since 1973, in 2000, an agreement was signed between the two countries to develop Ayodhya and Gimhae as sister-cities. In 2001, a memorial for the Indian princess was inaugurated on the west bank of the river Sarayu in Ayodhya. In 2018, the former first lady of Korea, Kim Jung-sook, visited Ayodhya and led the 'bhoomi pujan' (laying of foundation stone) for a new memorial of Queen Suriratna in Ayodhya. Many of our Korean friends visit Ayodhya and Bodhgaya, besides Delhi and Agra, when they travel to India.

Upon our return to India, a friend from Tamil Nadu added a new twist to the story. He said that the princess who went to Korea was from Tamil Nadu, by the name

Sembavalam. He added that some researchers have argued that the ancient name of Ayodhya was 'Saketa', and that Ayodhya is not near any sea or port for the princess to undertake a sea voyage.

Besides, there are some similarities between Tamils and Koreans. For instance, how they address their fathers as 'appa' in both languages and mothers as 'amma' (Tamil) and 'eomma' (Korean), both words being phonetically alike. Both communities are rice-eaters too.

All I can say is that Queen Heo Hwang-ok did go from India to Korea. I told my Tamil friend that today, if not in the past, Tamil Nadu has a connection with Korea, as there are many Koreans in Tamil Nadu, thanks to Hyundai's operations near Chennai.

Authoritarianism and Transition to Democracy

Syngman Rhee was the first president of independent Korea and served from 1948 to 1960. He went to study in the US, and due to his anti-Japanese activities, he lived there in exile for 40 years during Japanese rule. He was a pro-independence activist who had the backing of the US when he returned to Korea after its independence in 1945. He was at the helm during the Korean War and brought significant political and social changes in the difficult initial years. He had to resign in 1960 due to widespread protests by students and civic groups challenging his authoritarian style of governance. A democratically elected president proved to be short-lived, and a military coup led by General Park Chung-hee overthrew the civilian government in 1961.

Park Chung-hee's rule from 1963 to 1979 marked a period of tremendous economic growth and development, but it was also characterized by authoritarian control. He was a military officer during Japanese rule and had been influenced by their economic growth model. He was completely focussed on economic development and quashed all forms of dissent in a brutal manner.

When I asked my Korean friends about Park Chung-hee's contribution, it evoked a mixed response. Generally, the older generation was in awe and gave much credit for Korea's development to him. Some from the younger generation felt he was too authoritarian and suppressed the will of the people.

I asked my friend Mr Kim, who was in his late sixties, about his views about Park Chung-hee's contribution and his memories of the 1960s and 1970s. Kim was very well-read and had worked at a very senior level in companies in the Hyundai group.

'In the 1960s, when I was a child,' Kim told me, 'I remember my father telling us how President Park Chung-hee had galvanized the whole nation to get educated and work hard to make the country strong. No doubt he was an authoritarian leader – he governed with an iron hand and his famous words were, "Democracy can wait, let us have food on the plate." He was of the firm belief that political freedom can exist only if there is economic freedom.

'From the 1950s, land reforms had been implemented by the first president, Syngman Rhee, which aimed to redistribute land to tenant farmers, reducing inequality in rural areas. This virtuous cycle was continued by Park Chung-hee throughout the country. It helped improve agricultural productivity and led to a more equitable distribution of wealth.

'Korea was an agriculture-based country, but Park Chung-hee implemented a series of economic policies focussed on key sectors like textiles, chemicals, heavy industry and electronics. This helped establish a strong manufacturing base. The government invested heavily in infrastructure projects, including the construction of roads, railways, ports, bridges. These investments facilitated economic growth by connecting different parts of the country and improving logistical efficiency.

'My father's favourite story was how people criticized Park Chung-hee when he planned an eight-lane highway from Busan to Seoul when there were hardly any cars in the 1960s. Today, this 400-km road from north to south of the country is the nerve centre that has led to the development of so many towns on the way.

'The government identified a few businessmen and gave them certain sectors like construction, electronics, chemicals, automobile and ship building to invest in. Based on their performance, these businesses grew to become large conglomerates called "chaebols".

'The government actively promoted exports by providing incentives and support to businesses involved in international trade. Park Chung-hee realized that Korea is a small country with limited natural resources (most of the natural resources were in North Korea), and the only way to succeed was in the international market. Competing in the global market meant focus on quality, and success in international markets boosted the confidence of Korean businesses. This approach helped Korean companies gain a foothold in global markets and earn precious foreign exchange. Since foreign exchange was scarce, the Korean government had an arrangement with Germany whereby Korean women were sent to work as nurses and Korean men worked in the mines, and foreign exchange was remitted back to Korea. The general mood in the country was to work hard and contribute to the country's growth in whatever way possible.

'But let me tell you,' Kim continued, 'that all this development would not have taken place if the people were not educated and skilled. There was a thrust on education right from the 1950s, and the government gave top priority to human capital development as a crucial factor for economic growth and nation-building. Education was promoted at all levels, and the government invested in technical and vocational training programmes to provide a skilled workforce for the growing industries. The government promoted scientific research and technological innovation by establishing research institutions and providing funding for research and development projects.'

While Kim was narrating what President Park Chung-hee did for the country in full flow, I interrupted him to prod him about the abuse of power and the absence of civil liberties during that time.

'You know, it was needed then,' he retorted. 'When there is chaos and poverty, you need someone who is strict and is able to control the people. According to me, Park Chung-hee's biggest contribution was to bring about political stability after the chaos of the 1950s, which gave confidence to businesses both within Korea and internationally, and led to phenomenal infrastructural and economic growth.'

I spoke to some other friends too, and what they said about Park Chung-hee resonated with what Kim had said. While nobody doubts that Park Chung-hee's economic policies contributed to rapid growth and development, many felt that he did abuse power and brutally suppressed dissent.

This political stability was shaken in 1979 when Park Chung-hee was assassinated. Chun Doo-hwan, a military officer who rose up the ranks during President Park's tenure, was entrusted the task of investigating the assassination. He gave orders to arrest Army Chief of Staff General Jeong Seung-hwa for conspiring to kill President Park. This arrest was initially resisted. This led to a fight between two groups within the army, with Chun Doo-hwan taking control of the military. When martial law was established across the country in 1980, there were wide-spread protests (especially in the city of Gwangju) which were ruthlessly quashed by Chun Doo-hwan, and he continued authoritarian rule till 1988.

Pro-Democracy Protests and the Olympics

In June 1987, a year before the Olympics were to be held in Seoul, students staged mass pro-democracy demonstrations, which spread across the country. Some of my Korean friends who were in college or in their twenties during this period recounted their experiences and memories of this time.

Once, while walking with my friend Lee Soo-won in downtown Seoul, he turned to me and said, 'We are walking on these broad streets bustling with activity and so many vehicles today. When I was young, back in the 1980s, these streets and squares near City Hall, Seoul Station, Jongno Street and Gwanghwamun Square had very few cars. For months, thousands of youngsters like me would stage demonstrations to protest against the authoritarian regime to usher in democracy. Today, only old-timers like me will remember those days. I still get goosebumps when I think of them.'

I asked our friend Prof. Dae Ryun Chang, who is in his sixties, whether he had any memories of the demonstrations. 'I had just started my academic career in the business department at Yonsei School of Business in early 1987,' he told me. 'Demonstrations on the campuses were daily events that have been shown aptly in the movie *1987*. One of the key events during those demonstrations was the death of two students – one from Seoul National University and another from Yonsei, who studied in the business department where I taught. I went to his funeral and burial service that was held in Gwangju, where most of the business faculty went along with his corpse on a bus. When the bus reached Gwangju (the site of the infamous mass killings of demonstrators in 1980), the eerie silence of people looking sadly at the bus, welcoming one of their own back home, has stayed with me even after all these years.'

The Chun Doo-hwan administration did not want to use force to quell the protests, presumably under American pressure and the forthcoming Olympics. Roh Tae-woo, who became the leader of Chun's Democratic Justice Party, agreed to release political prisoners and hold presidential elections in December 1987. In 1988, Roh Tae-woo, who had been a military leader and a close ally of Chun Doo-hwan, was elected as the president in a closely contested election.

The year 1988 was an eventful one in Korea's contemporary history, marked by the successful hosting of the Summer Olympics and elections for a new president that paved the way for democracy.

The fact that Korea got an opportunity to host the Olympics in 1988 was, in a way, a recognition of its remarkable economic progress and was a sign of the confidence that the world had in its capability. As at any Olympic venue, preparations had to be meticulous, and Koreans were known by then to be excellent in execution. With the support of the government and the chaebols, Korea constructed state-of-the-art stadiums, transportation systems and accommodation. The global community witnessed Seoul's transformation into a modern and dynamic city. The Olympics also proved to be a platform for global unity and cooperation.

When we saw the K-drama *Reply 1988* on Netflix after our return to India in 2020, the student demonstrations and the excitement of hosting the Olympics depicted in the show seemed quite familiar to us.

Since the momentous year 1988, Korea has conducted presidential elections successfully, with every new president getting only one term of five years and striving to improve the democratic process. It may be noted that only a single term is allowed for every president, as per the country's Constitution, since 1987. Korea has a multi-party democracy, with two major parties having the most representation in the National Assembly that comprises 300 members with a term of four years. The voter turnout during elections is quite high – 77 per cent versus India's 65 per cent.

Among the later presidents, Kim Young-sam, the first civilian president, brought about reforms to bring in transparency in political funding and launched an anti-corruption campaign. Kim Dae-jung was known for his 'Sunshine Policy' of engagement with North Korea and won the Nobel Peace Prize for his efforts to promote peace in the Korean peninsula; Lee Myung-bak, former CEO of a Hyundai-group company and former mayor of Seoul, prioritized infrastructural development; and Park Guen-hye, daughter of former president Park Chung-hee, became the first woman president of Korea. Despite showing promise initially, her popularity started waning after the Sewol ferry tragedy, which people felt was handled badly by her government. Later, there was an uproar regarding a major corruption scandal. We gathered all this from conversations with friends.

Since this corruption scandal broke out while we were living in Korea, we got to see how the leaders were held accountable from close quarters. It was alleged that President Park Guen-hye's close friend had inappropriate access to confidential information and wielded her influence to extort money from chaebol owners to fund two foundations – one for culture and another for sports. When I discussed the corruption scandal with my colleagues, I was surprised to see the expression of strong sentiments. At first, I thought the amount involved is not that much and that nothing would happen. But protests started gathering momentum both on social media and on the streets, and in the end, President Park Guen-hye was impeached, removed from office and sent to prison.

One of my colleagues mentioned in a lighter vein that the Blue House (president's residence called 'Cheong Wa Dae') is jinxed. One president lost his life while in office and many have been sent to prison after their term, yet people want to become president. President Yoon Suk-yeol apparently has not lived in the Blue House since May 2022.

President Yoon, whose party is in the minority in the assembly after the 2024 elections, gave the country and the free world a scare at 11 p.m. on 3 December 2024 when he announced emergency martial law on TV. There was chaos, fear and anger for some time. The cabinet met within two hours and revoked the decision. To everyone's relief, the President had to withdraw his emergency orders within six hours. There were wide-spread protests calling for the President's resignation. Parliament passed a motion to impeach President Yoon Suk-yeol on 14 December 2024. As per the constitution, a constitutional court will decide his fate within six months as to whether he can continue in office or not.

An interesting fact about India and Korea's shared Independence Day of 15 August is that the date was not a coincidence after all. Lord Mountbatten had chosen 15 August as the date of transfer of power in India because it was an important date in his life; he was the commander of the Allied forces when Japan surrendered on 15 August 1945 and Korea became independent.

Given its serene mountains, clear, tranquil waters and green terrain – especially in the mornings – Korea came to be known as the 'Land of Morning Calm'. After weathering the storm of Japanese rule for over three decades and a three-year war, followed by three decades of authoritarian rule, today it is a vibrant democratic country.

Korea transitioned from authoritarianism to democracy, and economic development was achieved at phenomenal speed over the decades with progressive government policies, thrust on exports, rise of chaebols and a burgeoning educated middle-class. This phenomenon was dubbed by economic experts as the 'Miracle on the Han River'.

2

Miracle on the Han River

It is said that Korea's economic condition was worse than India's in the late 1950s and early 1960s. While India was in the process of nation-building after its independence in 1947, Korea was further impoverished and devastated by the Korean War.

How did its fortune change? How did Korea progress to a developed country within two generations, from a per capita income of less than USD 300 in 1970 to USD 35,000 in nominal terms in 2023? To give a perspective of what Korea has achieved in a short span of time, their per capita income (in terms of purchasing parity) in 2023 of USD 50,000 is higher than that of Japan (USD 46,000) and some European countries like Spain (USD 46,000) and Portugal (USD 42,000).

Based on my discussions with Korean friends, I found some similarities and many differences between Korea's and India's approaches towards nation-building.

First of all, one must remember that compared to India, Korea is a small, homogeneous country with a population of a little over 51 million – less than the population of an Indian state like Gujarat (72 million) or Karnataka (68 million). The people speak one language, and eat and drink similar food. India, on the other hand, is almost equal to 30 Koreas with the sheer range of languages, religious beliefs, customs and food habits. Managing India is indeed far more complex!

This does not in any way detract from Korea's achievement of literally rising from the ashes. While India embraced democracy since its independence, Korea experienced authoritarian rule for more than three decades. Like India, Korea had five-year plans for economic development. The plans chose specific industries for the allocation of capital as part of a comprehensive development strategy. But there was a major difference in the implementation of these plans.

The Indian government adopted a socialist model and the task of nation-building by way of major projects was undertaken by public-sector undertakings, with little accountability for efficiency and financial performance, some of which continue to be a drain on the country's resources even today. The trajectory of Indian economy might have been different had it focussed on private investment rather than the public sector for industrial growth; or in other words, if we had followed the US model rather than the Soviet one. But spare a thought. As a young nation struggling against adverse circumstances, it would have been virtually impossible for India to invite foreign capital for private investment. However, I do feel that we were suspicious of private-sector investments and remained a closed economy for far too long.

In Korea, President Park Chung-hee's government awarded key infrastructure projects to private businessmen, and rewarded efficiency and performance. The presence of the US military and its influence perhaps helped in this decision. Interestingly, President Park Chung-hee nationalized the banks in early 1960s, like it was later done in India, but the banks in Korea were privatized in the 1980s, unlike in India. The government directed the flow of capital through state-owned banks to targeted industries. With the domestic market in Korea being small, the thrust was on exports – which meant focus on quality to be competitive in the global market. To encourage exporters, tariff on crucial imported inputs were eased, which helped reduce the cost of inputs for the exporters and low interest-rate loans were granted and monitored closely.

Rise of Chaebols[*]

Chaebols are typically large, family-controlled conglomerates that have played a significant role in shaping Korea's economy and society. This business model was based on the Japanese 'zaibatsu' model, which was prevalent before World War II, and was done away with by the Allied forces to prevent concentration of economic power in the hands

---

[*]Reinhardt, Forest, Schlefer, Jonathan, Chi-Ho Wong, Keith and Yamazaki, Mayuka. *Korea*. Harvard Business School, 20 April 2015.

of few individuals in Japan. But in Korea, the government encouraged the growth of chaebols in the process of nation-building, and they continue to thrive and wield considerable clout till today.

When Korea became independent, the new government got ownership of many industrial assets set up by the Japanese. These were sold by the government at cheap prices to Korean companies like Samsung and Hyundai. Later, President Park Chung-hee allocated resources, such as capital and licences to operate in certain sectors, to these chaebols to invest in multiple sectors like ship-building, automobiles, electronics, chemicals, construction and finance.

A chaebol consists of a holding company with subsidiary companies in related or diverse businesses. Some of the top chaebol groups have affiliate companies ranging from 30 to 80 companies, with overall control exercised by the founder and family members through a complex arrangement of circular shareholding.[*]

Chaebols have diverse businesses, many of them vertically integrated so that the output of one company is sold to an affiliate company at an agreed-upon transfer price.[**] For example, Hyundai Motor Company buys powertrains from its affiliate firm Hyundai Transys, sells its spares and accessories through Hyundai Mobis, and the logistics is managed by Hyundai Glovis. The platform development for Hyundai and Kia models is in many cases

---

[*]Ibid.
[**]Ibid.

managed by a central team in R&D. All this leads to better control over the entire value chain and helps reduce costs.

Since the development from the 1960s to the 1990s was driven by government direction and incentives, most of the chaebols were naturally close to the political power centre and continue to remain so even today.

Chaebols are characterized by a highly centralized structure, with a top-down decision-making process. A central planning office that reports to the group's chairman acts as the control room for the group's businesses. It sets the direction, finalizes the business strategy, allocates resources and selects key managerial personnel.[*]

Of the many chaebols in Korea, I will talk about some of the major ones here.

Samsung was started by Lee Byung-chul in 1938 as a trading house during Japanese rule, and it expanded into electronics, ship-building, construction, insurance, retail and finance. Samsung Electronics is a major player in the global smartphone and semiconductors markets, and has today become a household name. It is the number one chaebol in Korea.

I graduated from being a Blackberry user to a Samsung mobile user once I landed in Korea. It took me time to get acquainted with the Korean currency, and the scale of operations, revenue and market capitalization of giants like Samsung. Once, one of our chief auditors from India was visiting us in Seoul. I mentioned to him that Samsung was

---

[*]Reinhardt, Forest, Schlefer, Jonathan, Chi-Ho Wong, Keith and Yamazaki, Mayuka. *Korea*. Harvard Business School, 20 April 2015.

setting up a new factory for semiconductor chips near our factory at a cost of nearly INR 1 lakh crore, which came to about USD 15 billion. His immediate reaction was, 'Can't be.' He thought I was making a mistake with a couple of zeros. I told him that the amount I had mentioned is what Samsung earns as profits in six months. He immediately said, 'Oh! Then it is possible.' Context was key in this case.

Hyundai group, founded by Chung Ju-yung in 1947 as a construction company, is known the world over for its automobiles. It is also actively engaged in ship-building, construction, retail and finance.

The automobile business comprises Hyundai Motor Company and Kia Corporation (which became a part of the group after the 1997 Asian financial crisis). Together, Hyundai and Kia enjoy about 70 per cent market share in Korea and have established factories around the world. They have a strong labour union that has greatly influenced the automobile industry, and was a source of constant comparison for SsangYong's labour union. Many senior personnel in our company had worked at Hyundai and we got to hear many interesting stories about what had led to their global success.

For example, Hyundai Motor Company initially test-marketed their vehicles in Canada and South America and faced quality issues, which were corrected over a period of time. Once they were confident about their vehicles, they entered the challenging, more demanding US market and introduced an ambitious warranty scheme to demonstrate confidence in their quality and brand. Americans could not pronounce 'Hyundai' properly, so the company ran a campaign to communicate that 'Hyundai' is pronounced like 'Sunday'.

My first association with Hyundai Motor Company was in 1998 when I purchased their car Santro in India. It was my first taste of reliable Korean quality.

The SK group, started by Chey Jong-gun in 1953, has made significant contribution to the energy, chemicals and telecommunications sectors, and is a leading player in the semiconductor industry. I got acquainted with SK Telecom when they were the service provider for my mobile when I reached Korea.

LG Corporation, founded by Koo In-hwoi, was earlier called Lucky-Goldstar. In 1995, it was renamed LG with the tagline, 'Life's Good'. Like Samsung, LG is a major player in the electronics and household appliances sector. LG has been actively engaged in the chemicals business, and is well known in Korea for its cosmetics and personal care products. It is a leading manufacturer of lithium-ion batteries, supplying to global auto makers, and is a global leader in the manufacture of display panels (OLED) for TV and smartphones. In India, LG air conditioners, washing machines, televisions and refrigerators are ubiquitous, including in our home.

The CJ group was originally a part of the Samsung group till the early 1990s. The grandson of Samsung's founder is the chairman of the group today. The CJ group has been a pioneer in the food business and has expanded to take Korean cuisine global. It has been active in the biotechnology space, and in the twenty-first century, it has been a leading player in the entertainment and media industry. With a focus on spreading Korean culture globally, it has played a significant part in nurturing Korean talent to make K-pop, K-drama and K-cuisine popular worldwide.

POSCO is one of the largest steel producers globally. Besides that, it has business interests in energy, engineering and construction. It was started by the government and not by a chaebol family. Today, it is a public company managed by professionals. POSCO attempted to enter the Indian market with a mega project in Odisha, but it did not fructify. It had signed a memorandum of understanding (MoU) in 2005 to set up an integrated steel plant, but due to protests by local citizens over land acquisition and environmental concerns, it withdrew after 12 years in 2017. In 2024, it signed a MoU with the JSW Group for an integrated steel plant in India. I had the privilege to visit POSCO's factory in Pohang, which was truly state of the art, with a nice museum showcasing their rich history.

The Daewoo Group in automobiles and ship-building and SsangYong group in textiles, construction and automobiles were big names till the 1990s, before they went bust during the 1997 Asian financial crisis. SsangYong Motor Company will be discussed in greater detail in Chapter 4.

In the twenty-first century, tech companies began to see a boom. Naver Corporation, with its popular search engine, Naver, became a leader in Internet services, while Kakao Corp. is today a mega business with more than 90 per cent Koreans using their messaging app. They are also involved in Internet banking services and a taxi hailing app (Kakao T), and their emojis are a craze with youngsters all over the world.

What is central to the success of chaebols is their involvement in multiple businesses, and their achievements in global markets. They have moved up the value chain every decade or two to invest in businesses for the future, and they continue to evolve.

It may be noted that family-owned businesses are to be seen all over the world – in the US, in Europe and we see so many of them in India as well. In Korea, some of these companies have become so big that they are seen to be close to the government and wield immense power, which many citizens feel should be checked.

Asian Financial Crisis (1997)[*]

In the 1980s and 1990s, some countries in Asia had pegged their currency to the US dollar. Capital inflows led to overvaluation of currency, and the system of fixed exchange rate became unsustainable. Excessive borrowing and decline in asset prices brought about financial instability. In 1997, Thailand experienced sharp currency devaluation and capital flight that led to a contagion across many other countries in Asia such as Indonesia, Malaysia and South Korea, along with a deep financial crisis.

Once Korea joined the Organisation for Economic Cooperation and Development (OECD) in 1996, its

---

[*]Reinhardt, Forest, Schlefer, Jonathan, Chi-Ho Wong, Keith and Yamazaki, Mayuka. *Korea*. Harvard Business School, 20 April 2015.

financial institutions got access to low-cost foreign debt. This led to Korean businesses going on a borrowing spree way beyond their equity holding. In late 1997, the Asian financial crisis affected Korea drastically, with the Korean currency (won or KRW) plummeting by more than 50 per cent. Foreign currency reserves depleted and the International Monetary Fund (IMF) offered a loan of over USD 50 billion, conditional on the Korean government's implementation of austerity measures and better governance with tighter credit policies. Whenever I discussed it with my friends, they referred to it as 'IMF Crisis', as though the crisis was caused by the IMF!

Historically, the working of chaebols lacked transparency. Minority shareholders had no voice, and accounting and auditing standards did not require full disclosure of information. No questions could be asked about capital allocation across the businesses within the group, creating excess capacity and giving suboptimal returns more often than not. Owners were shy of diluting their equity stake when easy credit was made available, so much so that the debt-to-equity ratio crossed 500 per cent in many cases in 1997.

The financial crisis affected all businesses, including the big chaebols. They were forced to restructure their businesses, merge business units with other competing units, undertake major layoffs, and sell assets and investments. The government initiated 'workout programmes', whereby banks gave loans and monitored the turnaround of companies. The companies had to write down their equity holdings and restructure their debt through debt-equity swaps, term extensions, rate cuts and other refinancing arrangements. The government infused billions of dollars through issuance of bonds to purchase non-performing loans and recapitalize financial institutions.

Many chaebols had to sell assets and issue equity shares to reduce the debt-to-equity ratio from 500 per cent to less than 200 per cent as directed by the government. Companies were required to ensure compliance with the appointment of independent auditors and international accounting standards. Minority shareholders' rights were enhanced and the practice of cross-affiliate debt guarantee was eliminated. More than 10 major chaebols went bankrupt, including Daewoo and SsangYong Motor Company, or were merged with other chaebols like carmaker Kia that was merged with Hyundai Motor Company.

The weak currency in 1997 gave an impetus for export to rebound and slowed down imports. This led to the current account deficit in 1997 turning into a comfortable surplus in 1998. There was privatization, opening up of the capital markets and a more transparent and competitive corporate sector. Koreans showed their resilience and the economy bounced back at the beginning of the twenty-first century. The consolidation and merger of chaebol businesses helped achieve scale and reduce excess capacity. Today, the chaebols remain powerful as ever, in close proximity to the government and owners of substantial assets.*

---

*Reinhardt, Forest, Schlefer, Jonathan, Chi-Ho Wong, Keith and Yamazaki, Mayuka. *Korea*. Harvard Business School, 20 April 2015.

As Korea became an industrial powerhouse, exporting to various countries, infrastructure development kept pace to improve the quality of life for citizens.

Impressive Infrastructure

The first thing that caught our attention when we reached Korea was the infrastructure. We landed at the impressive airport in Incheon, which stands out like the Changi airport in Singapore. No wonder these two airports vie for the top global honours every year. Airports in the US and Europe look very old and lack proper maintenance. Even Tokyo airport seemed below par in comparison to these two. I suppose, they all developed many years ago and have lost their sheen. Perhaps this is why even new airports in India look much better than the ones in the West.

So, what is so special about the Incheon airport? Yes, it is spacious, grand and clean, and has clear instructions and helpful staff. Checking in or getting out of the airport is smooth. Even if it is crowded, there is never any chaos. People seem to be patient and things move seamlessly. Most of the time, it took us less than 30 minutes to get from the aircraft to the car after going through immigration and collecting our baggage – there was efficiency at every step.

Once, it was the month of May and we were returning to Seoul from India. We had heard that mangoes could not be brought into the country, but we had not eaten Indian mangoes for a long time and thought, 'Let us take a few and test the Korean system.' The bags passed through the conveyor belt. At the exit, security dogs sniffed out the mangoes and we were stopped. With a heavy heart, we saw the mangoes being dumped into trash bins. Since this was a first-time offence, we were let off with a warning that next time our passports would be confiscated. Although we missed out on mangoes, we got proof that the system worked.

Another efficient system was the check-in system at the Seoul railway station. Our friends had some shopping and sightseeing to do in Seoul, before taking a flight to Seattle. They checked in their baggage and completed their immigration formalities at Seoul Station, came out and did their sightseeing and shopping without the burden of their baggage, and then took the train to the airport.

From the Incheon airport, one can take a train to Seoul Station and there are many buses called limousines that go to different parts of Seoul and other cities, cruising mostly at speeds of 100 km/hour. The airport is about 75 km from the main city, and for almost 65 km there are no traffic signals but only wide roads and bridges. What a drive it is! We cross the famous Incheon Bridge, which is 21 km long and built over the sea, and whizz past toll booths at 50 km/hour. The view is scenic, starting with the ocean, followed by green mountains with thick foliage and tall sky-scrapers nestled among them.

As one approaches Seoul city, one sees several bridges over the Han River connecting places from north ('buk') to south ('nam') of the river. To the north of the river are Seoul Station, Namsan Tower, Gyeongbokgung Palace, Blue House, City Hall, and other old establishments and markets. To the south of the river is Gangnam, a commercial district that became famous globally after rapper Psy's song 'Gangnam Style' went viral. Also in this area are the National Assembly at Yeouido, the Olympic stadium and later developments, including Lotte World Tower – the tallest structure in Korea and sixth tallest in the world at 555 m. Some of my friends who were from the older northern part mentioned how, not too long ago, Gangnam was overrun with paddy fields. It is now a busy, modern, commercial area where SsangYong had an office. The riverside is well developed with green parks for citizens to enjoy bicycling and walking or for families to camp during day time, especially on summer weekends.

Public Transport System

The true test of a good, developed city or country is its public transport system. Seoul is a big, busy city with an extensive metro rail network, mostly underground, with several lines connecting different parts of the city and suburbs. There are clear signs in Korean and English languages, and one has to be careful to take the correct exit. I used to go to Gangnam station often, and it took me a long time to get used to the 10 exits meandering through countless shops.

Many underground stations have big shopping areas comprising designer boutiques, restaurants, convenience stores as well as small shops catering to all age groups and budgets, and they all seemed to be doing roaring business. Some stations have direct access to prominent tourist spots, markets, big malls and five-star hotels. There are clean toilets in all these stations, and we missed this when we used the London tube. Contactless smart cards give access to the subway system, and we don't remember ever seeing a ticket inspector. Often, one can see volunteers offering help to foreigners and senior citizens.

In the bus system, there are separate bus lanes, and stops give details of bus timings and live monitoring, providing expected time of arrival of the next bus. Big vehicles carrying six or more passengers are allowed to use the bus lane, which helps traffic move faster. My colleagues would use such a vehicle to go to the factory and would reach half an hour before me. I remember using a seven-seater vehicle when we had guests from India, and they were so thrilled when we sped along the bus lane when there was a traffic jam in the other lanes.

While we could use the app for metro since it was in English, for buses, there was an app only in Korean at the time, and hence, we used it less often. There was a limousine bus from our residence to the Incheon airport and we used it sometimes. Buses were differentiated by colours with names like 'Gani', 'Lani', 'Rogi' and 'Tayo' – colour names in Korean to attract children. We were surprised when we came to know that our grandson was familiar with them because he had toy buses back in India that sported these names. Animation cartoons of these colourful buses are still popular among children, not only in Korea but also in other countries. This promotion motivated more and more people to start using buses.

For taxi service, people use Kakao app, which is only available in Korean, and hence we used it only occasionally from a taxi stand. Most taxi drivers speak only Korean. We would, at times, see some taxis with a board saying 'international taxi', which meant the driver knew English. We never had any bad experience or heard any stories about incorrect meter-charging. Taxi drivers are known to be very safe, and it is a common sight to see men and even women who might be intoxicated being dropped home safely by them at night.

Throughout the country, one can find broad roads with clear markings and signage as in any developed country. On some of the roads leading to small towns and villages, the signs are only in Korean and foreigners find it difficult to navigate these parts. Inter-city and express buses connect various parts of the country, and are efficiently operated. The rest areas on national and state highways have plenty of place to park vehicles and buses, a variety of restaurants, shopping areas, clean toilets and blaring loud Korean music lending a festive air to them.

The national railway system provides high-speed regular train services connecting major cities. The high-speed train KTX, from Seoul to Busan – which is comparable to the famous Japanese 'Shinkansen' – takes less than two-and-a-half hours to cover a distance of about 400 km at a maximum speed of over 300 km/hour. Korea has invested well in the public transportation system to ensure that it is efficient, clean, punctual and reliable.

Besides an efficient road and rail network, Korea has developed several ports, with Busan being the biggest. They have state-of-the-art technologies like automated container handling systems, and have also spurred related investment in logistics facilities. This has helped increase efficiency and reduce logistics cost so vital for an export-oriented country like Korea to be competitive in the international market.

Intelligent Urban Design

One of our favourite places in Seoul is the Cheonggyecheon stream. As Seoul was rapidly developing, a highway was constructed over the stream. While this was useful to manage traffic, the unintended consequence was that the stream became a dumping place for garbage, which made it a breeding ground for mosquitoes and affected the well-being of the residents.

In 2003, the then mayor of Seoul, Lee Myung-bak, who later became president, initiated a project to demolish the highway and restore the stream. The first priority was to purify the water. Lots of trees were planted along its length. Walkways and bridges were built for citizens to enjoy their walks. Historical exhibits were displayed on the walls, and cultural events were organized along the stream to foster a sense of community.

Now one can often see people relaxing with their feet in the water or walking on the cobbled stones on either side of the stream, appreciating the art and history of the king's procession displayed on the walls, with light folk music playing in the background. It is a brilliant sight around the Buddha's birthday, when the area is decorated with paper lanterns of different shapes and sizes. Today, Cheonggyecheon has become an attractive, accessible recreational place for not only citizens but also tourists.

While there is lot of talk about conserving the environment in the recent past, the restoration of the stream was indeed a bold move 20 years ago and deserves a thumbs-up for sensitive environment-friendly urban planning.

When Indian Prime Minister Narendra Modi visited Seoul in May 2015, he made it a point to visit this stream. I guess the restoration work was close to his heart, as he had implemented something similar in Ahmedabad along the river Sabarmati when he was the chief minister of Gujarat.

While the Cheonggyecheon stream was a bit far from our home, our other favourite place for a walk was a man-made stream near our house in Bundang. There was a 17 km-long track along the stream, which inspired us to go for walks daily for eight months of the year when the temperature was above 10 degrees Celsius. It was particularly a treat to walk during spring (cherry-blossom season) and autumn, when the trees displayed a riot of colours. There would often be music played by people exercising; there would also be equipment to exercise, a public swimming pool for children to cool off during summer and a toilet every 200 m. To add to the fun, some stones were laid in the water to help cross from one side to another, which children and adults enjoyed with the same enthusiasm.

It is not an overstatement to say that Koreans love to build bridges. Be it on the river Han or on the smaller streams, numerous bridges are built for easy access, some for trains or pedestrians and many for vehicles. What surprised us was that the administration did not hesitate to stop using bridges or highways if the need arose. For instance, in 2015, an important highway near the busy Seoul station was discontinued for vehicular traffic for safety reasons and to provide walking space to citizens. Since 2017, this bridge has been converted into a walkway for pedestrians, with a profusion of flowers and plants that made it look like an elevated garden. From this bridge, I counted the number of lanes from Seoul Station to the other side of the road and could not believe there were nearly 20 lanes. I have not seen such a broad road outside the main railway station anywhere else.

Koreans are particular about their physical health and like to exercise and trek. In a big city like Seoul, areas like Namsan, Bukhansan and Seoul City Wall have especially been developed for trekking. What I find creditable is that places are developed for citizens rather than for tourists. On any day, one can find so many citizens, especially senior citizens, trekking with a stick in hand and with proper shoes and kit. I went trekking a couple of times and thoroughly enjoyed the scenic views, fresh air, facilities and the overall experience. If the climb is steep, in some places there are steps on which rubber mats are laid out to avoid slipping when it rains.

While there are some very big parks – like Seoul Forest Park, Seoul Children's Grand Park, Yeouido Park, Songdo Park and many others along the river Han – every locality has smaller parks adjacent to tall apartments. A few kilometres from our house, there was the huge Bundang Central Park with neat walking and cycling tracks, fountains, ducks swimming, small bridges to cross over, reading facility and a 'hanok' with traditional Korean furniture and utensils to remind the young of the past. Further down was our favourite Yuldong lake, which had the bungee-jumping activity that we were not so keen to try. We came to know that bungee-jumping was not allowed for senior citizens when one of our friends from India was refused entry because she was over 60. I got a chance to walk on this frozen lake one winter.

When you get an aerial view, you see patches of green amid the skyscrapers. In fact, the forest cover of Korea is close to 65 per cent. As our daughter-in-law Divya once said, 'Korea is not just a concrete jungle; it is concrete and a jungle.' In many countries, gardens that are tourist attractions are used by the local citizens whereas in Korea, the local gardens for citizens seem to have become tourist destinations.

Korea presents a lesson in urban planning – how a new locality is developed, not focussing just on skyscrapers or apartments but also parks, schools, markets, wide roads, and public transport connectivity with buses and metro. I used to tell my friends in a lighter vein that there are two Koreas – not North and South but one below ground and one above. Below the apartments you have basement parking and shops, beneath the roads you have the metro, in the metro stations you have shopping complexes and restaurants, sometimes three to four levels underground. In fact, it could be a good strategy to use these basement establishments as bunkers in the unlikely event of a war or during natural calamities. I was told that, in the past, Koreans used to undergo a training in disaster management to handle emergency war-like situations.

Traditional and Modern

What I appreciate about Korean infrastructure development is how it is able to balance the modern with the traditional. While one can see the traditional tiled houses in rural Korea, some are preserved even in a big city like Seoul. The palaces and Buddhist temples are reminders of ancient architecture. Most of the parks have a resting structure using a traditional tiled design. As mentioned previously, there are places where the traditional houses called hanoks are preserved so that the younger generation is able to connect with the past. In fact, Bukchon Hanok village in Seoul is a popular tourist spot, so much so that the authorities are planning to restrict the timings after local residents complained of noise and disturbance.

A typical hanok will start with a courtyard. Its roof is sloping with tiles made of earth or kiln-fired clay. The wooden framework of the house is assembled without the use of nails, relying on a system of interlocking wooden beams. The doors and windows are made of 'hanji', traditional Korean paper that allows diffused light to filter through. The space below the elevated wooden floors is used for storage.

A distinctive feature of a hanok is the 'ondol' heating system. A network of pipes beneath the wooden floor carries warm air from a separate heating area, which could be a raised platform with a stone surface that provides a heated surface during the cold season. It is interesting to note that this principle of ondol heating is used even in modern skyscrapers, where heated water comes from central water heating stations directly into our taps through pipes laid under the flooring (just like gas and electricity) keeping us warm in winter. Our friends had one bad experience when they switched off the heater in winter, like we switch off lights, when they went to India for a few weeks. In this case, the pipes under the floor froze and cracked, resulting in major repairs. This was a lesson for all of us that this heating system is different, and we took utmost care to ensure that it was not switched off at any point during winter.

I would like to share one hilarious experience here. There would sometimes be announcements by the building administration in Korean, via speakers installed in each apartment, which one of our colleagues who did not know the language would ignore. Once, as he was having a shower, the water supply stopped. He waited for some time, then, with great difficulty, after wiping off the soap, he went down to enquire. The administration staff informed him in broken English that there had been an announcement that due to maintenance, there would be no water supply. After that, whenever there was any announcement, just to play it safe, he would run to fill a bucket!

After he told us this experience, we would also fill a bucket whenever there was any announcement. It so happened that once, when I was in office, there was an announcement, and Sudha, as usual, ran to fill the bucket. This was before she had learnt the language. After some time, a neighbour knocked on the door and urged Sudha to come down. The announcement was for a mock fire drill.

In India, people follow 'vastu' while designing a house. Similarly, hanoks are rooted in traditional Korean building techniques considering climate, available resources and maximizing exposure to sunlight, with the north side being used for the family and private rooms, and the south for communal and open spaces. When our son's family came to visit us, we went to stay in a hanok about 300 km from Seoul. There was plenty of room to park the car in the courtyard and play with our grandson. We slept on wooden floors with thin pillows barely supporting our necks, had dinner and breakfast comprising local cuisine on low tables while sitting on the floor, and experienced the warm hospitality of the family with whom we stayed. Then they showed us around their garden and bamboo trees, and gave us a glimpse of village life in Korea.

Waste Matters

Waste segregation is something everyone follows religiously. In our apartment, there were separate bins for paper, plastic, metals, glass and food waste – so much so that we had to remove the plastic or metal covers from the glass bottles and dispose them in their respective bins. We had a CCTV camera for monitoring purpose, and sometimes we saw the people who came to collect the waste, wearing gloves and the mask, reprimanding some people if they had neglected to separate the waste or had used the wrong bin. The bins and the room where they were kept were also well maintained, which prompted us to show this system to visiting Indian friends and relatives. Disposing unwanted household items can be expensive and one may have to pay for it. Many times, people would keep such items outside the trash room, with or without a nominal price tag and their phone number, for a fixed number of days. This was a well-established practice and we rarely found the same items for more than a few days, which meant that either some people took or purchased them or the owners disposed them on their own. There would be a box for old clothes, which would be donated to the needy periodically.

All this was a big change for us coming from India, where we have the raddiwala to collect paper and scrap dealers to pick up unwanted things and get some value out of it. Once, our mixer grinder had stopped working, and we looked for a shop where it could be repaired, only to be greeted with blank, surprised faces. It seems such items were not repaired in Korea but were disposed of. Similarly, the zip of our suitcase could not be repaired. Sudha insisted that we take the mixer grinder and suitcase to India and get it repaired there rather than throwing them away.

We did that and are still using the items. We later understood the philosophy of not repairing, especially electronic items – the models are upgraded every year and people prefer to buy new models rather than repair old ones. It was no surprise then that we also got influenced and changed our mobile phones every two years.

The practice of segregating waste and disposing it in appropriate bins is seen throughout Korea – be it in offices, apartments, old houses, restaurants, shops and parks or other public places. In public places, we find three bins: for food waste, recyclables and general waste. There is a separate bin to dispose pet poop bags. In a public park, we were surprised to see a designated fenced area for pets to play without a leash and a provision of boxes of pet poop bags and tissue paper, in case someone had forgotten to carry them.

Our Korean friend Cecillia Kim told us that her father, Kim Jung-wi, was the environment minister in 1995. One of the initiatives introduced then was the concept of waste segregation and management. It is no accident that today we see people follow this habit of cleanliness and waste disposal across the country. This is the result of public awareness campaigns (using TV and print media in the past, and now social media too) and educational programmes that aim to inform citizens about the importance of waste segregation, the adverse impact of improper waste disposal on the environment, and the benefits of recycling.

Waste segregation is mandatory at the source, and non-compliance can result in fines. Some areas have introduced smart waste bins that track and monitor waste disposal, thereby helping better waste management planning by municipalities. Korea has invested in e-waste collection centres, advanced waste treatment facilities, recycling plants and facilities that generate energy by managing non-recyclable waste effectively. Public education, strict regulation and investment in technology have made Korea a leading player in sustainable waste management practices.

Citizen-Friendly Governance

Being used to dug-up roads with the sign 'work in progress' and the perennial construction activity in India, Korea offered a pleasant change. I used to jokingly tell Sudha,

'This country looks completely ready as if nothing is left to be done.' Then we gradually realized that there is work happening but without disturbing normal life or traffic, keeping the noise and dust levels under control. Where we were staying, we had noticed some activity happening in the next apartment complex, but before we knew it, a multi-storeyed building had come up. A 200 m road in front of our apartment building was re-tarred within a day. We had witnessed some trucks coming but were surprised to see they had a system of cleaning the truck tyres before leaving so that the roads were not affected with tyre marks. There was hardly any noise or disturbance. We came to know later that they used a lot of pre-fabricated material; hence, the speed of construction.

Wherever we went in Korea, we got a sense that the administration cares for its citizens, especially for the elderly. Most public places are disability-friendly. Citizens above the age of 65 are given free passes for public transport. The ubiquitous free public toilets are a solution to the 'natural problem' of Korea's growing number of senior citizens. Clean toilets can be found within 100–200 m of metro stations, parks, markets and other public places. In fact, sometimes, we felt that there was a competition to show which toilet was the best. They are decorated with framed photos, plants and flowers, and we could not help but take some pictures to show back home. And we are talking of ordinary public toilets, not the ones in malls that were anyway like in a five-star hotel.

Well-stocked convenience stores, be it E-Mart or GS or 7-Eleven, are found at every nook and corner. When it rains, most shops keep plastic covers in a rack outside, and people can insert their umbrellas in them so that water does not drip all over the place. If you go to the beach, there will be a place to wash your feet when you come out, and at golf courses, there is a compressed air facility to remove the grass from the shoes when you come off the course after playing. A seemingly simple idea we liked were the big umbrellas at street corners installed to protect pedestrians from sun, rain and snow.

We were impressed with the ease with which we got our driving licence and Alien Registration Cards from government offices in our first month in Korea. Some brief paperwork and we were done in half an hour.

Korean Growth in the Twenty-First Century

Thanks to the progressive economic policies and their effective implementation, and in no small measure to the success of the chaebols, the country saw almost double-digit growth for more than three decades till the 1990s. This is why some economic experts call this Korean growth story the 'Miracle on the Han River'.

While manufacturing and infrastructure development continue to be Korea's forte, the beginning of the twenty-first century shifted the focus towards a knowledge-based economy, emphasizing research, development and innovation. Samsung, for instance, became a leader in smartphones and semiconductor manufacturing, while LG made strides in consumer electronics and home appliances.

The twenty-first century heralded the growth of the Internet and 'soft power'. As the government's focus for the new century turned to innovation and technology, Korea became one of the early adopters of broadband Internet. The country is known to have one of the highest speeds of Internet connections in the world. This has enabled the growth of online services and e-commerce. Free or low-cost Wi-Fi connectivity is available at public places including in airports, railway stations, restaurants and public transportation.

Korea was a pioneer in mobile technology, thanks to giants like Samsung, LG and SK Telecom, and was one of the first countries to roll out 5G. Their advanced mobile infrastructure led to a plethora of services including streaming and gaming. Due to high-speed Internet network, the video game industry took off, with many young Koreans becoming avid gamers – so much so that video games became a spectator sport with crowds thronging to big stadiums to watch their stars play on the big screen.[*] Video-gaming became popular worldwide, earning Korea billions of dollars by way of exports.

What we appreciated was that Koreans developed and used their own apps. For example, most of them use KakaoTalk rather than WhatsApp; instead of Google search and Google maps, they use Naver search and Naver

---

[*]Reinhardt, Forest, Schlefer, Jonathan, Chi-Ho Wong, Keith and Yamazaki, Mayuka. *Korea*. Harvard Business School, 20 April 2015.

maps. Uber is struggling to penetrate the taxi market dominated by the locally developed Kakao Taxi.

The IT development also had another positive cultural impact in the area of entertainment, with the global popularity of K-pop music and K-dramas. Sudha had a better experience of this soft power called K-wave, and I will let her share her experiences.

Hallyu: The K-Wave

At the beginning of the twenty-first century, the Korean government started actively promoting its cultural exports as part of its soft power strategy. The key components of Hallyu are K-dramas, K-films, K-pop and K-beauty.

Till 2013, we were happy watching Hindi, Marathi and English movies and serials on Indian TV, and there was no OTT platforms, at least in our lives.

In Seoul, when I started learning Korean, I met a Japanese woman named Keiko in the class and became friends with her. She introduced me to a famous Korean TV serial called *Winter Sonata* (*Gyoul Ryonga*), which had released in 2002 and had become very popular, not only in Korea but also in Japan and other surrounding countries. I began watching this K-drama with English subtitles to practise my Korean-language learning, and got hooked to it. According to Keiko, the Japanese loved *Winter Sonata* for the romance – the ladies loved the hero and there was a joke making rounds that Japanese women were getting divorced because they were comparing their husbands with the Korean hero.

I liked the drama so much that I recommended it to Vasudev, who enjoyed it – especially the theme song, which was enchanting, but did not find anything special about the hero for the Japanese women to fall all over. Later, we both liked visiting Nami Island, where the first kiss in the drama was shot amid winter snow. It has now become a popular tourist spot.

In 2015, we got an opportunity to go to Harvard Business School for a one-week training programme arranged by Mahindra & Mahindra. One of the case studies mentioned a famous TV serial called *Jewel in the Palace* (*Dae Jang-geum*) from 2003, which had not only become very popular in Korea but had also been exported to many countries and garnered a significant viewership. Since this was part of the case study, I started binge-watching this serial and got to understand and appreciate the historical atmosphere of the palace, women wearing traditional Korean hanbok, cooking traditional Korean dishes for the king and other important officials in the palace, the rivalry, the jealousy, the love story that unfolds and the opening track that used traditional Korean folk music. It was all mesmerizing!

Later, I started watching Korean series on TV without subtitles, which helped me improve my Korean and colloquial diction, and also allowed me to converse with my Korean friends about them.

The first time I got a sense of the popularity of K-dramas in India was in 2017, when I had come back to get away from the harsh winter of Korea. Vasudev had to visit a dentist in Mumbai and I had accompanied him. The dentist made a passing mention to his assistant, a young girl doing her internship, that we had come from Korea. The girl jumped from her seat and was very excited to talk about Korean series and her favourite hero, Lee Min-ho. Both of us were surprised to know that there are young fans in Mumbai watching Korean serials. But a bigger surprise awaited me the same afternoon.

I went to visit a friend who worked as a helper in the school where I had previously worked, and as we were talking about my Korean experience, her teenage son got interested and made a call to his college-going cousin in a remote village in Maharashtra.

He said, 'A madam from your favourite country has come to our house. Speak to her.' He then handed me the phone.

The girl at the other end greeted me with 'annyeonghaseyo'. I was pleasantly surprised. Then she continued in Marathi: 'Madam, my friends and I like Lee Min-ho a lot in Korean dramas. We are learning Korean on YouTube. I want to study in Korea, we like Korea very much because of the Korean series.' She then asked me many questions about life in Korea, which I answered.

I advised her: 'Study hard and get a job first. Earn your own money or get a scholarship and then think of going to Korea to study. Korea is an expensive country and even if you study in Korea, it might be difficult to get a job there. Be prepared for that.'

That day, I realized that the popularity of Korean series was not limited to big cities but had extended to villages where access to the Internet was a challenge.

A few months before we left Korea, I was in Seoul when, one afternoon, I got a call from a friend in India.

'Hello Sudha, please explain to my daughter that in the 12th Board examinations, they will not ask questions on Korean series! Since you live in Korea, you would know why this generation is so obsessed with Korean series.'

I did the usual counselling, but I am not sure how far I succeeded. I have heard this sort of complaint from many Indian parents.

Vasudev saw only one serial when we were in Korea, *Winter Sonata*. All this changed once we shifted back to India during the Covid-19 lockdown. He had just retired and we could not go out anywhere. There were only phone calls and Zoom meetings, and OTT platforms were in great demand. As I started talking to my friends about what programmes to watch, I was surprised to learn that most of them were watching Korean serials. Here I was, trying to leave behind Korea and settle down in India, and my friends were taking me back to Korea!

For a few months after shifting back to India, we would watch Hindi and English series and movies on OTT platforms. But whomever I spoke to seemed to be into Korean dramas, and as a result, I would often feel left out in the discussions. Although I had seen many TV series while in Korea, I suggested to Vasudev that we start watching Korean series together.

The first K-drama we saw in India was *Itaewon Class*, which covered our favourite place in Seoul (Itaewon) and reminded us of the pubs and restaurants that we frequented. It revolved around a restaurant in Itaewon and the detail in which daily life was depicted, especially the drinking and eating, made us nostalgic. Thanks to the subtitles, Vasudev could follow the story, though he would get annoyed with me when I pointed out mistakes in the subtitles.

After *Itaewon Class*, we moved on to *Reply 1988*, which captured the time when the Olympics were held in Seoul, the student demonstrations to usher in democracy, the daily lives of ordinary people, parents' aspirations for their children's education and, of course, the food that they cooked at home then (in contrast to the eating-out culture that prevails today).

The next series was *Crash Landing on You*, which was about a rich South Korean girl who, while riding a balloon, lands in North Korea and falls in love with a North Korean soldier. What we found amusing was that some North Korean soldiers at the border were shown watching South Korean dramas illegally because they were banned in the country.

Some of our other favourite series were *Descendants of the Sun* (a romance involving a soldier and a doctor) and *Inheritors*, which focussed on the super-rich and how some spoilt school children looked down on others, along with showing proxy wars for the control of big companies. Further, *Sky Castle* dwelt on the sensitive topic of coaching classes and the mad race to excel academically, which many Indians would relate to because of the competitive mindset of Indian parents and children.

Squid Game became a rage worldwide and revived an old Korean children's game, but in a different, gruesome, spine-chilling form. While in any regular game the loser gets eliminated, this high-stakes game brings out the greed and desperation in human beings, where the participant stands to lose his or her life. *Extraordinary Attorney Woo* portrayed the life of an autistic lawyer brilliantly. In *Dr Cha*, a doctor goes back to her profession after raising her children and faces innumerable challenges in doing so. *Prison Playbook* was set in a prison, and told the stories of prisoners with different backgrounds and professions, including a baseball star. Before we knew it, we were hooked on K-dramas!

What makes Korean series so popular? The content is undoubtedly great. As mentioned in an *Alzajeera* article, 'While the language, setting and characters are distinctly Korean, the way they are crafted is actually quite global in its sensibility and is meant to be palatable to international audiences. K-dramas' appeal lies in their "emotional stickiness". Indians can particularly relate to the appeal of South Korean culture.'* The quality of production is top-class and each episode seems to promote Korea as a country.

Every series conveys a message and touches on sensitive topics, while at the same time showing daily life in Korea. Most of them end after one season of about 16 episodes and at a point when you want more. I would always feel sad and there would be a vacuum for some time after a series ended. The best of Korea is projected, since this is an export product. The greenery, the mountains, the Han River

---

*Sharma, Suparna. "K-Craze: Korean Dramas and Culture Are Taking India by Storm." *Www.aljazeera.com*, 15 September 2021, tinyurl.com/mryhvt3z.

at night, life in the city and countryside, the attractive cast and, of course, the cuisine – all make for engrossing content.

In most movies made in any part of the world, one only sees actors entering a restaurant, maybe ordering some food. But in Korean series, one will see in detail what they have ordered, how they eat and drink, and the names of the Korean dishes. This, I feel, is a conscious strategy to popularize Korean food, and I must say that they have been quite successful. 'The sale of ramyun noodles increased in India by 178 per cent in 2021 compared to the previous year, and there was a 3.5 times jump in sale of K-beauty products in India, not by any marketing or distribution plan but influenced by K-dramas!'

'Influenced by K-dramas and K-pop, young people in India are learning the language not for employment but because they want to understand what their idols are saying, what the singers are singing. They want to have a direct connection with Korea through the language.'[*]

The icing on the cake was when the Korean movie *Parasite* won several awards including one for best film at the Academy Awards in 2021.

Before going to Korea, we had a glimpse of K-pop when, in 2012, Psy's 'Gangnam Style' became a rage all over the world. Everyone from global leaders to celebrities began tapping their feet and riding an imaginary horse to that catchy music. Psy, till then famous only in Korea,

---

[*]Sharma, Suparna. 'K-Craze: Korean Dramas and Culture Are Taking India by Storm.' www.aljazeera.com, 15 September 2021, tinyurl.com/mryhvt3z

became an overnight global sensation because, thanks to social media, the music video had crossed 1 billion views on YouTube in less than six months. This demonstrated the potential of digital platforms in shaping global trends, and the unparalleled scale that can be achieved with its reach across the globe – transcending boundaries, languages and cultures. This song not only propelled Psy but also K-pop on the global stage.

When we asked our friend Prof. Dae Ryun Chang about the success of 'Gangnam Style' and K-pop, we realized that it was no accident. There was a strategy in place and many years of hard work on the part of the Korean entertainment industry, supported by government policies to make K-pop into the multi-billion-dollar industry that we see today.

In an article on *Harvard Business Review*, Prof. Chang, along with Kyongon Choi, states

> Girls' Generation, a tandem of nine young pop singers and dancers, became a YouTube sensation with their song 'Gee'. Their popularity, not only in Asia but also on other continents, led to their fans holding flash mobs in cities like Paris and Los Angeles, where crowds would emulate their idols' dancing. But it's not the music itself that caused the sensation. Instead, it is how the groups were using marketing and cultural outreach to gain attention.
>
> The key secret to K-pop's success is the use of a well-crafted Culture Technology (CT), a concept developed

by Lee Soo-man, founder of SM Entertainment, the largest talent agency in South Korea. SM Entertainment and other similar outfits have succeeded in designing and seeding Korean pop culture in foreign markets to expand their global appeal.

These talent agencies resemble old Hollywood studios in terms of their size, organization, contractual relationship with their stars and control of their private lives. Each agency has hundreds of young talents who are trained as quadruple threats: they can sing, dance, act, and speak foreign languages. But where the older CT model relied on local artists … the updated model tries to embed more and more foreign singers from strategic markets into larger girl or boy bands. These imported singers are then used to promote their acts back in their respective home countries.

And this goes a step further. Girls' Generation and its male version, Super Junior (which contains 11 singers), are sometimes broken into sub-units with each specializing in different aspects of entertainment whether it is singing, dancing, rapping, or language. In effect, they become like a 'Transformer' that can be configured and then reconfigured into different cultural versions. For instance, Super Junior M ('M' for Mandarin) is a sub-unit that was developed specifically for the large Chinese market.

CT even goes so far as to assign foreign composers, producers, and choreographers to be used for certain songs to expand the cultural outreach. The intended result is that the look, sound, and feel of these songs are 'local' regardless of where they are played. Thus, K-Pop transforms into 'U-Pop,' or universally popular music.*

Companies like SM Entertainment, HYBE, CJ ENM, YG Entertainment and JYP Entertainment, scout, train, manage and promote artists to help them achieve international recognition. They also help artists collaborate with internationally popular musicians, which results in fusion and variety. Music festivals and concerts help extend their reach.

There are many K-pop groups, some of the most popular being all-boy bands BTS and EXO, and the all-girl group Blackpink, that have become household names around the world. BTS burst on the scene in 2013 after the 'Gangnam Style' fever caught on, became famous in Korea and captured the attention of an international audience when they started winning in various categories of the American Music Awards, 2018 onwards. All members of the group are very active on social media and have a huge fan base, which calls itself 'ARMY'.

In India, there are K-fan clubs in towns and villages, apart from in the big cities. The Korean government makes a focussed effort to monitor Hallyu in different countries so they can strategize accordingly. For instance, the Korean Cultural Centre in Delhi, with the Korean Embassy's help,

---

*Dae Ryun Chang and Choi, Kyongon. 'What Marketers Can Learn from Korean Pop Music.' *Harvard Business Review*, 21 July 2011, tinyurl.com/y6tuevnt.

supports Hallyu fan clubs' activities, and regularly conducts K-pop music and dance competitions. Trophies and trips to Korea go to those singers and dancers who copy K-pop idols with precision, matching every move, every beat, even attire.*

I was not a K-pop fan, but there was a lot of buzz when BTS won the American Music Awards in 2018. We were in Korea at the time. I came to know more about BTS when my nephew Naren and his wife Deepika came to visit. Deepika told me that she wanted to shop at a BTS franchise store for her teenage nieces from Darjeeling. We went to the store in Insa-dong and found a profusion of posters, T-shirts, jackets, keychains, wallets, water bottles, boxes and many other items with pictures of the members. Deepika made a video call to show her nieces the store and the souvenirs. They were so excited and knew the names of the artists and had their own favourites. 'Jimin looks so handsome! Jungkook is so good!' they exclaimed.

Our next destination was a Kakao store in Gangnam. Although I had been using the KakaoTalk messaging app, I only came to know about the store, thanks to the teenagers from Darjeeling. It was a huge store, selling mostly their emojis as souvenirs. The Darjeeling teenagers were giving us instructions on what to buy over video call and I was left wondering what a Korean wave this was.

---

*Sharma, Suparna. "K-Craze: Korean Dramas and Culture Are Taking India by Storm." *Www.aljazeera.com*, 15 September 2021, tinyurl.com/mryhvt3z.

Koreans are also beauty-conscious. When our teenage nephew came to Korea, he was floored by the pretty Korean girls. He used to say, 'How can their skin be so soft?' It had never occurred to me, but I began to notice that indeed, both men and women had flawless complexions. Since I had never used any make-up, I was not aware of the trends and fashions, and assumed it must be the natural nature of their skin. One day, I asked a Korean friend what the secret of Koreans' complexion was and she explained, 'There are many skincare products in the market developed by Koreans which help keep the skin healthy and radiant. All the stars of K-pop, K-dramas and films use these products and endorse them. Naturally, everyone wants to look like their idols.'

Korean skincare products cater to the young as well as other age groups. Hence, their use has become universal. Thanks to the success of K-dramas and K-pop, amplified by social media and online shopping, Korean cosmetics have attracted international attention and become popular globally. Apart from Korean stars, beauty influencers and bloggers also promote Korean cosmetics and skincare products on YouTube and Instagram, reaching a global audience.

Whenever we had guests from India, it was my job to take them shopping. Thus, I came to know that Amorepacific is a Korean company and not French, with famous skincare brands like Innisfree, Laneige, Sulwahsoo and many more – which my Indian guests happily tried and bought. On my own, I had never been to a cosmetics store.

Once, one of my friends from India said that her daughter-in-law had asked for certain products from the Innisfree store. So, we went to one at Gangnam, where I learnt that Korean face masks, skin whitening creams, anti-wrinkle creams, mascaras, lipsticks, nail polishes, false eyelashes, artificial nails and so on are top quality. Seeing their radiant skin, I was sure the pretty sales girls would have used these products. They tirelessly showed us different products and if they convinced us to buy some of them, they would offer a freebie, which is called 'service'. I enjoyed this part of closing the deal, using my Korean language skills, and my Indian friends were ever grateful for the 'service'.

Given this profusion of products, I was surprised when my hairdresser asked me one day, 'The colour of your hair is so good. What do you use?' I replied, 'I use henna.' He continued, 'Can I get some henna packets to try on other clients?' I gave him some packets that I had, and he was very happy when I said that they were a gift from me. The next time when I went to him, he told me excitedly that his clients liked the henna, and requested me to get more packets from India. After that, whenever I visited India, I would gift him henna packets. When some of my Korean friends came to know of this, they said, 'Unni, get some henna for us too.' That solved my problem of what to get my friends from India other than scarves, cottons and accessories.

Beauty is given so much importance in Korea. It's not just cosmetics and skincare. Medical tourism is a big industry too. I was told that there are more than a thousand clinics in Gangnam district alone that offer cosmetic surgery. I asked my friend from the Gangnam tourism centre about this obsession with looking good.

'Koreans like to look beautiful,' she said. 'There are many well-qualified and skilled doctors who are good at performing eyelid surgery and nose jobs. There are well equipped clinics with excellent facilities to stay. Initially, it started for Koreans, but the government and medical industry promoted cosmetic surgery in countries where the potential was high. Now many international tourists come to Korea for cosmetic surgery.'

I said, 'No wonder so many Koreans look beautiful with all this cosmetic surgery and use of skincare products.' My friend quipped, 'When you see your good-looking favourite K-pop and K-drama stars promoting cosmetics and medical procedures, I am sure it influences the general public, not only in Korea but also globally.'

The government has supported this growing trend in medical tourism by facilitating easier access to international patients. I was told a large number of Chinese people come to Korea for medical procedures, and that one can see them shopping and wheeling big suitcases outside major markets.

While cosmetic surgery constitutes a major part of medical tourism, Korea also has expertise in other fields of medicine such as dermatology, dentistry, orthopaedics and ophthalmology. We even met some doctors from India who had come for a one-year advanced training in their field of specialization.

When we went to Seoul in 2023 to meet our friends, I was surprised to see Indian families on the road, not with a travel company or a group but by themselves exploring the city. We asked some of them what brought them to Korea because there were not many travel companies taking tours from India to Korea. One man said that his wife watched Korean series and wanted to see the country; another said his teenage daughter was a BTS fan and insisted that they travel to Seoul; and a third had seen so many Korean series that the family wanted to experience what they saw on screen and try out the Korean cuisine. None had come for cosmetic surgery, I might add!

Historically, the Koreans have lived in the shadows of their dominant neighbours, China and Japan. Because of this, Koreans were late to realize their cultural potential on the world stage. It is only in the last two decades that we have seen their confidence grow, after they have effectively shown the world, and themselves, how to conquer hearts with soft power.

The Miracle on the Han River can be attributed to strong leadership, a clear vision, detailed planning and speedy, effective execution, with a focus on education and continuous skill development. This requires an inspired and diligent workforce. How did this happen?

For that, we need to understand Korean culture.

3

'Uri Nara' Mantra

It is human nature to generalize based on observations and experiences, though in the same breath we say that every person is different. With Korea being relatively smaller in size than India, and quite homogeneous in terms of language, food and culture, it might be easier to generalize for Koreans than for Indians.

One characteristic that stands out when you meet and talk to a Korean is the 'country-first' approach. Everything else is secondary. All their actions seem to be guided by the 'Uri Nara' (our country) mantra.

National Pride

National pride is evident in the behaviour of all Koreans. I suppose it comes from mandatory military training that Korean men undergo before starting their working career. Men in the age group of 18 to 28 have to join military service for a period ranging from 18 to 36 months. This is applicable to all except those studying abroad or ones with medical issues. We were surprised to learn that the K-pop group BTS has taken a break since December 2022, so that the members can serve in the military. You might be earning foreign exchange in millions for the country but you are not exempt from military service. As Indians, we would find it commendable, but Koreans will say, 'So what? All of us have to go through the training.'

Sudha had a Korean friend whose son was studying in the US and would have been exempted from military training. Instead, he came to Korea, did his military training, went back to the US to complete his education and returned to Korea to join his father's business.

During our time in Korea, Sudha would teach at the Korea Dyslexia Association as a volunteer. One of our friend's sons went there to practise his English skills and helped Sudha in the class. Then we were told he had taken leave because he had enlisted for military service.

Four months later, Sudha's friend got a call from the military training centre that her son had met with an accident and was admitted to a military hospital. It was quite serious, and after surgery, the boy remained in the hospital for over two months. Sudha's friend took her son abroad to rest and recuperate. The military training centre processed an exemption for the boy, in view of the mental trauma he had undergone. His readmission to college was also in process. However, the boy had other ideas. He insisted that he would complete his training. His parents were supportive of his decision.

When Sudha asked the boy why he was going back after such a serious accident, he said, 'Imo, it was my fault. I did not follow the procedure to cross the barriers carefully and paid the price. Now, I want to go back and make amends.' Sudha was flabbergasted. I still remember when she came back home, she said to me, 'What fighting spirit this boy has. And so happily he wants to go back to the military training centre after a major accident!'

National pride is evident, especially when it comes to Koreans' interaction with foreigners. For example, whenever someone said anything negative about a fellow Korean, Sudha's Korean friends would immediately say, 'There must be some misunderstanding', or 'She did not mean it that way'. Once, when Sudha was travelling with her friends in a bus, her Moroccan friend, who was pregnant but did not appear so due to her loose dress, had to stand in the bus for some time. One of their Korean friends, while getting down, apologized saying, 'Nobody offered you a seat in the bus today. On behalf of my fellow Koreans, I apologize.'

When it comes to doing business, Koreans are very competitive among each other. But when there is a foreign competitor, they prefer to support the locals. Whenever we explored doing business with Indian or other non-Korean suppliers, it was interesting to see the advocacy on behalf of Korean suppliers for reasons like quality and logistics, even when the cost was not competitive.

Respect for Elders

In keeping with Confucian principles, Koreans hold the elderly in great regard. Young children are taught by parents to respect elders. If we ever happened to cross paths with a toddler with parents in our apartment's elevator and gave a smile, the parent would invariably ask the child to do 'insa' and the child would bow if standing and even if he or she was in their parents' arms. It was an adorable sight!

Since housing is very expensive in Seoul, we found many instances where aged parents lived with their married children and grandchildren, and took care of the grandchildren. Sudha met a senior citizen who told her that she got an allowance from her son to look after the kids from Monday to Friday, and that on weekends they went out for lunch or dinner. We had some friends whose parents lived separately but nearby, and there were many whose parents lived in small towns outside Seoul and the children visited them occasionally, especially during Lunar New Year and Chuseok.

As in Japan, the bowing culture is prevalent in all walks of life in Korea. While getting introduced, while leaving or saying goodbye, it is common to see juniors by age or designation bowing to their seniors. In formal events, before giving a speech, I would bow to the audience as per the Korean custom. At times, we would see photographs in newspapers of a senior official of the government or a CEO of a company offering a public apology by bowing down in all earnestness to take responsibility for any wrongdoing or fraud.

Just as age is respected, so is hierarchy, which we will discuss in the next chapter.

Age Is Not Just a Number

'How old are you?' This is a common question in Korea, especially among older people, which Sudha faced more often in the absence of a business card. This is because Koreans decide how to address you depending on whether you are older or younger.

When we revisited Seoul in 2023, I met some of my Korean friends over dinner one evening. One of them remarked, 'You know what? I am going to be one year younger from next month and Mr Lee will be two years younger.' I asked him, 'How?' He continued, 'The government has decided to adopt the international age system from 28 June 2023.'

Korea has traditionally had a different system to calculate age. A person turns one at birth, and thereafter, one year is added on the first day of every new year. For example, Sudha's friend's child was born on 25 December, and in February, after the Lunar New Year, the baby was deemed to be two years old! While Koreans were used to this traditional age counting method, it became very complicated while speaking to foreigners. Sudha's friends were happy with the government's decision, as they now felt younger!

Discipline

Thanks to the mandatory military training for men, discipline, it seems, comes naturally to most Koreans. Discipline is inculcated at an early age by parents at home and teachers in school. Keeping public places clean, disposing trash in designated bins, cleaning up pet waste, smoking only in designated areas – all of this is followed diligently by everyone. It is then no surprise to see Koreans waiting patiently in queues in shops or at bus stops. During our six-year stay in Korea, Sudha and I don't remember a single incident where anyone tried to jump a queue or made a fuss, even when it involved indefinite waiting.

I was especially impressed with discipline on the road, whether it was people who were driving or crossing the road. Most people follow lane discipline while driving. Honking is rare, and only to convey if someone has made the mistake of changing lanes without signalling. When I asked a colleague about this culture of no honking, he smiled and said, 'We used to honk just like you honk in India, but gradually it improved. I don't remember when we stopped honking.'

While going to my factory, we had to take the Gyeongbu Expressway, which we could see from our apartment. After about a month of taking this route, one day, 10 minutes into the ride, I told my driver Jay that the apartment we were passing looked just like ours. He said that it was indeed our apartment. Till then, I had not known that it took more than 10 minutes to pass our apartment on the expressway. The point being, there was a long detour to hit the expressway and one could take no shortcuts. On our way back from the factory, I was amazed to see Jay following the queue almost a kilometre long to take the right turn, when there were three other lanes almost empty where the cars sped straight past us. That is discipline.

I love to drive in India, but because of this strict discipline and driving on the right side of the road, I drove only a few times in Korea. Even then, I had Jay by my side and could not muster enough confidence to drive on my own. In spite of this road discipline, there would occasionally be an accident, but we rarely saw any shouting or frayed tempers.

In case of minor accidents, the drivers or owners involved would get down from their vehicles, take a photograph of the damage, call up the insurance company and move on. It is customary to keep a distance of 8 ft between two vehicles while stopping due to traffic or at a signal. I tried to follow this when I returned to India, only to find two scooters and an autorickshaw filling the 8 ft gap.

Punctuality

With discipline comes punctuality, which is practically a given in Korea. I realized that life can be very easy and less stressful if everyone is punctual – no waiting, no waste of time. People can plan their activities better. Once punctuality becomes a habit, there are no excuses for being late. No traffic jams, no sudden changes in schedule. Everything moves with clockwork precision.

In the office, all activities were planned meticulously, leaving no room for chance. Meetings started and ended on time most of the time. There was clear communication for changes in schedule, if any. I was surprised initially as to how people managed to be exactly on time. If a meeting was at 11 a.m., the person will come exactly at 11 a.m. even if they come from 50 km away. Then I came to know that the person reaches well before time, waits outside and enters at 11 a.m. On the other hand, before going to Korea, I had a different experience of punctuality in India. Although as a company we were improving time management, one could not expect punctuality in many cases, and we complimented people who came on time. The joke in India used to be that the trouble with being punctual is that there is nobody present to appreciate it.

Once, the Indian Ambassador had invited four Indian couples to his residence for dinner at 8 p.m. Since we were staying about 30 km away, we started early to reach the area about 20 minutes before time. I asked our driver to drive around a little to see the surrounding area while we waited. We reached the Ambassador's residence five minutes before 8 p.m. and waited outside. In those five minutes, three other cars came with the other Indian couples. At 8 p.m. sharp, I rang the bell and we all entered the residence together. I told Sudha, 'See, we Indians can also be punctual like the Koreans. It is just a mindset. And we should be consistent.'

We would always try to be punctual, but after our experience in Korea, we have become somewhat paranoid about it and are impatient when others are not on time. There have been innumerable cases after our return to India, where we have reached on time only to find others entering 30 minutes to 1 hour later. There seems to be no respect for others' time and one cannot plan well with such uncertainty.

Safety

When we moved to Seoul in 2013, North Korea was threatening to fire its missiles, and this news was read by many in India. Many friends and family members were worried and called us to enquire whether we were fine. To our surprise, there was not much tension in South Korea. The English newspapers gave little coverage, and it was business as usual. When I checked with some friends, they said that the North Koreans keep making threats, but nothing would happen. Then I came to know that all citizens have been trained in the past for war-like emergencies to take shelter in bunkers and underground subway stations. The fact that there are so many American soldiers in South Korea and a male population that has had military training gives them the confidence that the country is ready to face any eventuality.

To be safe and feel safe is the foundation of Korean life. We met many Koreans who returned after staying overseas for several years. When asked the reason for their return, they would only say, 'We feel safe in Korea.' After living there for more than six years, Sudha and I also experienced this feeling of extraordinary safety. Whenever we have travelled to other countries in the recent past, we have compared them to Korea and came to the same conclusion that Korea, Japan and Singapore seem to be the safest places in the world.

Safety is not just about law and order but also the quality of infrastructure and care for human lives. In India, we are so used to major mishaps where lives are lost. We read or watch the news about train and road accidents, bridge collapses, landslides, floods, fires, stampedes and serious crimes, and we move on. There may be some noise in the media for a few days, and then we do not really care about the root cause or the action taken against those responsible (which is seldom). In Korea, the quality of infrastructure is good and accidents are quite rare. More importantly, one gets the feeling that human lives matter and the focus is truly on ease of living.

During our six-year stay, there was one major mishap where more than 300 people lost their lives. This happened on 16 April 2014, when the ferry MV *Sewol* capsized on its way from Incheon to Jeju Island. Of the 476 passengers and crew on board, 304 lost their lives, including 250 students from a single school on a field trip. The whole nation was shocked, angry and in grief.

Later investigations revealed that the ferry was modified to carry more cargo and passengers than it was meant for, which had affected its stability. Besides, on the ill-fated voyage, the load was far in excess of what was permissible. This aggravated the effect of the sudden turn of the ferry, affecting the balance, which supposedly led to the ferry capsizing. To make matters worse, the rescue operations were slow and the captain and many of the crew members were the first to leave while passengers were advised to 'stay put'. In a country where the culture is to obey the orders of elders, most students did not move. Unfortunately, those who followed the instructions were not able to come out while those who bravely jumped were rescued.

As it became clear that this was a preventable tragedy, caused by negligence and breach of regulations, citizens took to the streets out of rage and grief. People were critical of the captain's and crew's inaction, and there was anger at the ferry operator/owner and the regulators. Government authorities tried to downplay the gravity of the tragedy, which angered the public even more.

The rescued vice principal of the school that lost 250 students, who had organized the field trip, died by suicide. After months of investigation and court hearings, the captain was held responsible and awarded a life sentence, while 13 other crew members and some from the ferry operator company received a maximum sentence of 12 years. The families of the victims were not satisfied with the investigation or the court verdict. They formed a group called 'Sewol Families for Truth and a Safer Society', and with the help of activists they have been trying to pressurize the government for the last 10 years to bring about systemic improvements to prevent such disasters in future.

This was the only big mishap in Korea during the first two decades of the twenty-first century. Unfortunately, another serious tragedy – by way of a stampede – happened in our favourite neighbourhood (Itaewon) close to Halloween, on 29 October 2022. We had been there in the past during Halloween. There are narrow lanes and alleys with trendy nightclubs, bars and restaurants frequented by foreigners as well as by local citizens.

Our Indian friend, Sachin Satpute, who lives in Itaewon, close to the scene of the tragedy, told me later that he was at this place with his wife just an hour before the tragedy occurred. Seeing the huge crowd, he had decided to go back home. As the crowd increased, there was no place to move and some groups started pushing, which led to people falling over each other with no route to escape. The ensuing stampede killed over 150 people, mostly young people and some foreigners, and injured nearly 200 people. The large crowd in the narrow lanes made access difficult, as ambulances and other means of help could not reach on time. The crowd for Halloween festivities had surged in 2022 because it was the first time that Covid-19 restrictions had been lifted after two years. There were early warning signals, like requests to boost the police personnel to control the crowds, which had not been taken seriously. People were angry with the police and the administration for their negligence.

Following the catastrophe, there were candlelight protests in many parts of the country. A week of national mourning was declared by the President. Flags in government offices were ordered to fly at half-mast. Memorials were set up in various cities. When we went to Seoul in 2023, we visited the memorial at Itaewon and could sense the gravity of the tragedy.

These unfortunate accidents remind us that even if a city has the best infrastructure and safety systems in place, there could be negligence or breach of regulations, for which accountability has to be fixed and action taken, if not by the government then by vigilant citizen groups.

Generally, whenever I browsed through English newspapers in Korea, I hardly found any news about serious crimes. On the rare occasion of a serious crime being reported, it would become a hot topic of discussion throughout the country. For example, there was a case where a person stabbed a woman in the crowded Gangnam Station one evening. It turned out that the accused was mentally imbalanced. Koreans were shocked and there were discussions for days about this incident. When Sudha spoke to her friends in the Seoul Police, they lamented that such incidents tarnished the image of the country and its security system.

In general, one feels safe even late at night while walking on streets or travelling through public transport. Many times, Sudha took the metro quite late in the night but never once felt scared or unsafe. It is a common sight to see people, including women, being helped into a taxi after a party, where one sober person will give the address to the taxi driver, who will then take the passenger to the designated place and hand them over to the apartment security, who in turn helps the person reach home safely. We did not hear of any cases where passengers were taken advantage of.

Nor did we see or hear of eve teasing. In fact, Sudha's friends told her that one is not supposed to stare at a lady for long if one wants to stay out of trouble. Once, while walking on a busy street, we saw a foreigner clicking pictures of a young girl. A passer-by, a local resident, noticed this. He went up to the foreigner, checked his phone and forced him to delete the pictures. We were truly touched by this care and concern displayed by a stranger, a vigilant citizen.

Sudha took these safe conditions for granted, so much that wherever she went, either to a shop or to a restaurant, she would leave her purse on the counter or table and look around. Not once did she have a bad experience during our six-year stay in Korea.

Once, Sudha went with her friend Christine Choi to the Express Bus Terminal underground shopping complex. There were hundreds of shops in that complex and they went into one of them. As Christine was buying something for her daughter, Sudha left her purse on the counter and started looking at the various items on display. Once Christine was done with her shopping, Sudha helped her with the bags and forgot her purse on the counter. Because she had some cash, metro card, credit card and house keys in her mobile cover, she did not miss the purse until she reached home.

When she realized that she had left the purse in the shop, she quickly did a recap of its contents and decided that she would let it pass, since the shop was very far from our house. Additionally, as she had not seen the name of the shop, it would be almost impossible to find it in that crowded market. After about three weeks, her friend Helena called up, and when Sudha mentioned to her that the lipstick she had given as a gift was lost with the purse, Helena immediately said, 'All lost things are in the lost and found office of the market. You should go and get it.'

Sudha asked her young friend Radha to give her company, and as they reached the market, Sudha started looking for some signs of familiarity but in vain. She then started looking for the lost and found office. As she was checking the map on her mobile, her friend Radha entered a shop to buy something for her daughter, and called out to Sudha.

Sudha followed her into the shop, and for no apparent reason, she said to the shopkeeper, 'I had left a purse three weeks ago in this market...' And before she could complete her sentence, that lady opened a cupboard and took out the purse and brought it to the counter as if she had been waiting for Sudha.

Sudha started rattling the contents of the purse: KRW 200, 000 (about USD 200), a lipstick, a water bottle and some other things. The shopkeeper simply crossed her hands, gesturing 'No need to tell me', handed over the purse with a smile and bowed graciously as Sudha thanked her profusely with 'gamsahamnida'. Sudha took a picture of the purse and messaged Helena, 'Found it.' Pat came her reply, 'Good that you went all the way to find it. In Korea, one normally does not lose things, and if you do, you will find it.'

Concern for Others

One quality that we came to greatly appreciate in Koreans, is their care and concern for others. This is expressed through their actions like respecting others' time and privacy, not honking on the roads, not speaking on cell phones or speaking in hushed tones in buses or trains.

Once, when Sudha had sprained her ankle, she called up a friend living in our apartment building to ask if she knew of any nearby clinic. At that time, this friend was in a hospital to take care of her son after an accident. She immediately offered to come and pick Sudha up and take her to the hospital where her son was admitted.

Sudha said, 'Don't bother to come. My sprain is not so serious. If required, I will call you again.' Later in the evening, her friend called up to enquire about Sudha's foot, notwithstanding the fact that her own son was in the hospital. She came to visit the next day and advised Sudha to rest, and refused her favourite cup of masala chai that Sudha offered to make.

At the beginning of our first winter in Korea, we had to set the temperature of the central heater in our house to 24 degrees Celsius but did not know how to, since the instructions were in Korean. Sudha asked our Korean neighbour if she could help. Our neighbour had come back from California and, hence, was able to converse with us in English. She said that she would send her husband once he was back from work. The husband came after 10 p.m. and helped us set the desired temperature.

Typical of Sudha, she asked him for another favour – whether he could explain how to operate the toilet seat buttons (ultra-modern to us), especially how to run warm water in winter since, again, we could not understand the instructions that were in Korean. Our neighbour duly obliged. In mock seriousness but with a smile, he asked Sudha, 'Anything else, Madam?' Sudha was quick to seize the opportunity and asked him, 'Can you please help me write a Korean essay about myself? I have to submit it tomorrow.' He laughed and replied, 'How can I write about myself for your homework?' Eventually, he sat and helped her write 10 sentences in basic Korean at 11 p.m. That was the start of a new friendship with our neighbours. Later, we were embarrassed when we came to know that he was the CEO of a company and had been humble enough to help us with mundane things that night.

At the convenience store near our house, Sudha had a habit of looking around after completing our routine shopping, while I stood in queue with the items purchased waiting to make the payment. Once, when I was in the queue and only two or three people were in front of me, Sudha noticed a brand of biscuits someone had purchased and asked the lady in which section she could find them. I was getting restless, since it was our turn at the counter next, while Sudha was off searching for the biscuits. She could not find any. The cashier at the counter had started preparing our bill when Sudha came and told her in Korean that the particular biscuits were out of stock. I got irritated and told Sudha in Marathi, 'Is this so urgent? The bill is ready, so many people are waiting behind us, let's go.'

But the cashier had different plans. She left the billing halfway, went to the biscuits section, confirmed they were indeed out of stock and requested Sudha to follow her to the warehouse in the escalator. She then came up with the biscuits, added them to the bill and asked Sudha, who was opening her purse which she had left at the counter, 'Are you happy now? We don't normally run out of stock. Apologies for the inconvenience today.'

Of course Sudha was happy! She was, in fact, thrilled and thanked the cashier for going out of the way to help her. I was quite embarrassed because the biscuits were not that important, and there were nearly 10 people waiting patiently behind us. But not a single person complained when the cashier left the counter. I am not sure if this behaviour is typical of all Koreans, but they are predisposed to ensure that non-Koreans view their country in a positive light.

Once, a couple came to visit us in Seoul from India. Sudha gave them clear directions from the airport to our house, the bus number from the airport, where and how to book the bus ticket, and the stop number where we will receive them. Our house was about 75 km from the airport, and being an express limousine, the bus had limited stops. There were no stops for the first 70 km, and the stop at our house was only the second stop. We were quite confident that our guests would reach safely and on time, since many others had done so earlier. But this time it was different.

Our friends managed to board the wrong bus which went in a totally different direction. To make matters worse, their mobile phone was not working. They managed to get help from a Korean bus passenger who knew some English. He called Sudha and gave the news that the bus in which our friends were would take them 50 km away from our house and that there were no stops in between. We had no clue where this place was and how to reach there. The good Samaritan told us not to worry and that he would get down at an appropriate stop to make sure our friends boarded the right bus to our place.

As soon as he helped them onto the next bus with all their luggage, he called up Sudha and told her that he had instructed the bus driver about the exact stop and that he would share the bus tracking map with her. Then, just before the bus arrived at our stop, he called up Sudha to ensure we were there to receive our guests, since he had been tracking the bus's progress as well. As we welcomed our guests and were unloading their baggage from the bus – two hours later than expected thanks to the goof-up – one Mr Kim, for virtually taking the responsibility for our guests' safe arrival. Our friends got their first taste of life in Korea and saw how helpful citizens can be when someone is in distress. We were all relieved that the ordeal was over, and as we settled down and joked over a glass of beer, I pulled our friend's leg, saying, 'Tell me, how did you manage to get on the wrong bus after all the details Sudha had sent?'

Balancing Process-Discipline and Relationships

Koreans have an affinity for doing things systematically, be it at the workplace, their homes or anywhere else. They do so by clearly defining processes in detail and following them. A lot of time is devoted to planning so that the execution is flawless. This ensures consistency in the quality of products and services. The downside of this is rigidity in approach.

One of our favourite stories is about the time when our friend Shashi Maudgal had gone to a Korean restaurant that served fried eggs. He had asked for an omelette but was promptly told 'eobseoyo', meaning 'don't have', with crossed hands. After experiencing Indian flexibility or 'jugaad' in most of the things we do, this was difficult to digest. After all, how difficult would it be to whip up an omelette from the same eggs that were being fried? But it was a matter of following systems and processes, which could not be compromised.

While on the one hand, processes are strictly followed, on the other hand, we also see many things getting accomplished by building and nurturing good relations. In such cases, one can work around processes without breaking the rules. In the above example, perhaps, my friend could have got his omelette if he had developed good relations with the people at the restaurant.

In Korea, business negotiations with suppliers and clients, as well as talks with government officials, are mostly concluded over soju and dinner. This trend is changing gradually with the younger generation. The government has also brought in restrictions on entertainment expenses and gifts to government officials, which can come under close scrutiny.

Once, a senior official of the company where I was on the board of directors, invited me to lunch at a fancy restaurant. I thought it was a courtesy call, and we talked about general things most of the time to get to know each other. At the end, he brought up a topic that I had raised in a board meeting, and started giving clarifications as to why what I had asked could not be done. I got the point and told him that he could have come to my office to give this explanation or even made a phone call. Then I remembered how much Koreans value relationships and prefer to close sensitive points over lunch or dinner.

Education, Sports, Hobbies

One of the main reasons for Korea's phenomenal growth is its focus on literacy and education, ever since the Korean War in the 1950s. Due to the emphasis on education and skill development, almost everyone in Korea is literate. A large majority of students enrol in universities, making Korea one of the most highly educated countries in the world. The importance of education is drilled into the minds of the young at an early age by parents, grandparents, teachers and neighbours.

Like in India, children are taught to be competitive, and parents are busy ferrying their children from one coaching class to another after school. These coaching classes are called 'hagwon'. In fact, some of them have their own buses, which is very helpful for working parents, and they also enable children to spend time with their friends on the commute. Once, Sudha had gone to meet her friend Christine, whose daughter was to be picked up from school. The daughter, who studies in New Zealand for a few months every year to improve her English, wanted to go with her friends in the bus for her extra English classes just to spend more time with her friends.

The pressure on children in Korea is not just for studies. In our apartment complex, we would see children carrying guitars or some other musical instrument entering the elevator around 10 p.m., totally exhausted. Supermoms, as Sudha calls them (or Tiger Moms, as they are called by Amy Chua), want their children to excel in studies, music, dramatics, sports. Thanks to this focus on studies and extracurricular activities, Koreans could relate to some Indian movies like *3 Idiots* and *Taare Zameen Par*, among others, which fared very well in the Korean market. Volunteering for a social cause is also quite common in Korean society, and starts from an early age. School students are encouraged to take up volunteer activities like keeping their surroundings clean.

Every year, on a particular day, there is a common entrance test for high school students, which determines which university they can join. On this day, one of the parents takes leave from work to accompany the child to the exam centre. We were surprised to learn that flights are rerouted or rescheduled during exam time, so as not to disturb the students. There is a mad race to get admission in one of the top three universities – Seoul National University, Korea University and Yonsei University – all of which are in short called 'SKY'. Proud parents will heave a sigh of relief if their children get admission to one of these three. If they don't, it is like the end of the world. The pressure put by parents and society has a telling effect on the students!

In our office, the first question to the HR department to vet job applications would be, 'Which university?' There is an inherent bias towards the top three, just like we have in India for IITs or IIMs. Almost their entire education is in Korean, and we found many youngsters making a special effort to learn English. Some who can afford it take the trouble to go to the US, Canada, New Zealand or Australia to get more practice in English speaking.

Koreans inculcate a reading habit from childhood, again mostly Korean books. An Indian journalist friend remarked that when he visited bookstores in Korea, there were thousands of international books translated into Korean. This gave Koreans access to a wide range of subjects from the best of authors. Kyobo is a popular bookstore chain, and their flagship store in Gangnam occupies a whole building with well-catalogued sections and reading facilities for customers like a public library. They conduct promotional events and a monthly 'meet the author' event. Our favourite was the Starfield Library in Coex, Gangnam – a massive facility where books were stacked across more than three floors and attracted local readers as well as tourists.

Korean literature got a boost in 2024 when Han Kang was awarded the Nobel Prize for literature. Her win has facilitated a massive increase in sales of not only her books but also other Korean authors and revived interest in reading (which was seeing a decline in recent times) – something that is being called the 'Han Kang effect'.

In the country of Samsung, it is not surprising to see Koreans, especially the young, clicking pictures happily and posting on social media. One can hear the familiar 'hana, dul, set' followed by 'kimchi' (like we say 'cheese'), and the giggling of the group as they make heart signs with their thumbs and index fingers. If a formal group photograph is being taken at office events, it will have everyone clenching their fists and shouting 'fighting'. Whenever we travelled outside Korea, Sudha would get excited if she heard 'hana, dul, set' and immediately go and talk to the Korean tourists and help them click more pictures.

Many Koreans pursue a hobby and make it a point to pick up a sport. Taekwondo is Korea's national sport. It is a martial art form that trains students to use attack and defence skills with their bare hands.

Football is a popular sport in Korea, with the Korean team doing well on the world stage – their best performance was finishing fourth when they hosted the FIFA World Cup jointly with Japan in 2002.

Baseball is also very popular, and the annual league draws record crowds year after year. Many Koreans play tennis, badminton, table tennis and volleyball. One sport I enjoyed watching was the annual foot-volleyball competition in our factory, where employees practised hard after office hours and vied for the top honours in front of the CEO and other seniors.

Golf has become quite popular among men as well as women, thanks to some Korean professional golfers like Yang Yong-eun and K.J. Choi in men's and Park Sung-hyun and Chun In-gee in women's categories winning PGA championships. The country has some wonderful golf courses as well as driving ranges and indoor golf simulators at convenient locations for people to practise.

One of the external directors on the board of our company, a professor, was a singer in an ensemble and played the guitar while his wife played the drums. Sudha and I attended one such programme and enjoyed their performance.

My interpreter would cycle to office about 20 km once a week in summer and was the proud owner of a very expensive bicycle, which she would bring into the office through the elevator. Our CEO went mountain-biking with his wife on weekends at the age of 70. Our R&D head pursued archery and won competitions. Some enjoyed skiing in the harsh winters.

With this sporting culture, it is not a surprise that Koreans generally are among the top 10 medal winners in

Olympic Games. In 2024, at Paris, they finished eighth with a medal tally of 32 that included 13 gold, 9 silver and 10 bronze.

Generally, we got a feeling that Koreans are health-conscious; they exercise and eat well. It was hard to find an overweight or obese person in Korea. One can find equipment for exercise in the various parks being diligently put to use by citizens who have come for a walk. On weekends and holidays, young parents take their children trekking in the mountains, swimming in public pools, or putting up a tent on the beach or at a park along the river Han.

Kimchi, Coffee and Soju

Koreans take their food seriously. And after watching K-dramas and YouTube channels, it seems they also want the world to take Korean food seriously.

Mukbang, which first started in Korea around 2010, has today become a rage world-wide on YouTube and other social media platforms. Mukbang (which literally means 'eating broadcast') are eating shows where the host consumes food, usually in large quantities, in front of the camera and also interacts with the audience. These shows started as live-streams but many are now pre-recorded. Viewers who may be feeling lonely or stressed like to watch the show while eating their meal, as if they have company while eating. Some people feel that the large quantity of food consumed (or supposed to have been consumed) on screen may lead to over-eating and wastage if the viewers try to emulate the host.

Sudha had many friends who did not cook at home but almost always ate in restaurants. The first thing that may come to mind is that it is not healthy to eat outside regularly. But it is not so in Korea. Most Korean restaurants serve healthy, clean, nutritious food, cooked the way you would make it at home. Many are mom-and-pop restaurants where the women of the family are in control. They are quite affordable and convenient, considering that you don't have to cook the variety of dishes or clean the various bowls and plates. Besides, if the spouses eat at the workplace and the children eat at their schools or colleges, there really isn't much need to cook everyday meals at home.

Every morning, Sudha's group of Korean friends would decide on their KakaoTalk group where to go and what to eat. Unlike in India, where most restaurants serve a wide variety of cuisines (some running into more than 300 items), in Korea restaurants are specialized and most of them serve a limited variety. For example, one will find restaurants serving only chicken or only pork or only beef or only seafood. In that, there could be further specialization of only barbeque, or served with rice and soup. What will be common in all restaurants are side dishes ('banchan'), which are usually served in unlimited quantity and are not charged for separately.

There will be the mandatory kimchi – cabbage fermented in pepper and/or fish sauce, garlic, roasted and sesame-coated seaweed flakes, seasoned soybean sprouts, boiled green vegetables, radish and cucumber soaked in vinegar, dried fish and so on. Just like in India, where annual pickle-making was a big event in the good old days and maybe even today in some parts, in Korea, annual kimchi-making is a big event where all family members chip in, so much so that I remember some of my colleagues asking for leave to help their families in this annual task! I understand that due to climate change, growing cabbage has become a challenge in many parts of Korea, and that may pose a risk to kimchi's future.

We got our first taste of the popular bibimbap on our first flight to Seoul. We were told that we could get vegetarian bibimbap. We saw all the Korean passengers having bibimbap so we decided to try it too. We got our bowl with steamed rice, on top of which we had to add the sautéed vegetables. It was quite bland. Then we saw the other Korean passengers opening tubes, pouring its contents on the rice and vegetables, and mixing it all up. We were told that this spicy red pepper paste, called gochujang, is the main ingredient. We mixed it, and was it spicy! I did not like the taste in the beginning, but over a period of time we gradually developed a taste for it, since this was the nearest we could get to vegetarian food in Korea.

Once, during our first few months in Korea, we had gone to Seoraksan ('san' means mountain) National Park on a Tuesday, when Sudha usually fasts or has vegetarian food. Our driver Jay assured us that we would get vegetarian bibimbap outside a Buddhist temple. As we collected our bowls, Sudha was surprised to see fried egg on top of the rice. We came to know that it was standard practice to add fried egg to bibimbap. When Sudha said she could not have egg on a Tuesday, Jay coolly removed it and offered her the bowl, not understanding the significance or sensitivity of a vegetarian. We were surprised when we were told that they could not serve bibimbap without the fried egg topping. Sudha decided to fast on that Tuesday.

When we went to Seoul in 2023, Sudha requested that the bibimbap be served without the egg topping. Same story – 'We cannot do that.' After lot of coaxing, the lady agreed to bring the egg in a separate plate, but the dish would be charged at full price. We did not mind that. At least, this time, Sudha could have her bibimbap without the egg.

I was a chicken and fish eater before going to Korea, and so was able to manage eating out, although the taste was quite different. Sudha was a vegetarian, but over a period she gradually started having soups, stews and seafood when she went out with her Korean friends. My favourite Korean dish is 'dak-galbi'. It is chicken barbequed at your table, and mixed with dak-galbi sauce, sweet potato and cabbage. I liked the taste maybe because of that sauce but the best part were the leaves in which you put the chicken, wrap it around and then eat it almost like a paan!

Then there was 'samgyetang', a chicken soup for which three hottest days in summer referred to as 'sambok' were designated. They varied each year and most Koreans had samgye-tang on those days. I went out with my office colleagues at least once a year at sambok and enjoyed the taste of samgye-tang, which was quite like sweet corn chicken soup that we get in India. I found that many people, especially youngsters, enjoyed fried chicken with beer in the evenings. Here, KFC would mean 'Korean fried chicken'. They called it 'chi-maek', short for chicken and 'maekju'.

We could not and did not eat what Koreans relish the most, which are dishes made with beef and pork. 'Bulgogi' is a delicacy Koreans will die for. It is a grilled dish made from marinated beef. At some of the formal sit-down dinner events that I attended, steak was served as the main course and there would be no other choice. I settled for side dishes and wine.

Seafood was widely available, and I enjoyed a variety quite different from what we get in India. I remember in my second month in Korea, when I was to go to Busan, our CEO suggested that while there I should try the raw fish for which Busan is famous. I came home and asked Sudha, 'How can one eat raw fish?' We went to Busan, saw raw fish in the market and in restaurants, but did not feel like trying it. After about a year, I started enjoying eating raw fish with my colleagues. It is called 'sashimi' and goes well with soya sauce. It is similar to the Japanese sushi but without the rice.

Once, my colleagues told me that they would take me to a special seafood restaurant. I asked them what was so special about it. One was the price; it was expensive. It served a special type of fatty fish that has an element of poison in it. The chef has to be an expert to serve it right for the perfect taste. I was not as excited as they were, and was glad to have survived the meal.

Another time, Sudha and I went for a drive with Jay to a beach, and on our way back we stopped for lunch at a place that was famous for serving live shrimps. It was quite a sight! Live shrimps were brought in and roasted with salt over a stove. We lost our appetites and ordered rice and soup. Jay, of course, feasted on the roasted shrimps. Near my office in Gangnam, I liked eating fried salmon with side dishes for lunch. Many times, when we had seafood soup or stew, I would joke to Sudha, 'They are serving whatever has come in their fishing net.' I could not make out the various items in the soup other than shrimp, squid, clam and weeds.

Sudha's favourite was 'haemol pajeon', a Korean seafood pancake, and 'japchae', a stir-fried dish made with sweet potato glass noodles and vegetables.

Korea has its share of street food, which Sudha enjoyed with her Korean friends more than I did. Places like Myeongdong, Insadong and Namdaemun in Seoul are famous for their street food. In the evenings, the streets are lined with vendors who do roaring business. Some of the popular street food items are 'tteokbokki', spicy rice cakes cooked in red pepper sauce; 'eumog', a type of skewered fish cake; 'kimbap', rice and vegetables or meat rolled with seaweed, which looks like Japanese sushi; 'keranpang', Korean egg bread; 'mandu' or dumplings; roasted chestnuts called 'gunbam'; and roasted sweet potato called gungoguma. 'Gungoguma' was my go-to food when we stopped at rest stops on sojourns outside Seoul; Jay would feast on his favourite roasted silk worms.

What I liked at the restaurants was the systematic arrangement of keeping chopsticks and spoons in drawers attached to the table. I would always have to ask for forks because, even after more than six years, I could not get used to eating with chopsticks, something Sudha was quite comfortable with. In some restaurants, where the speciality was a particular type of stew to be had with eggs, the raw eggs were kept in a drawer attached to the table along with the chopsticks. You could help yourself to as many eggs as you wanted by adding it in the stew, no questions asked. And if you wanted something else, you could give a shout, 'Yogiyo' and members of the staff would come running. If the staff were elderly, you addressed the lady as 'ajumma' and the gentleman as 'ahjussi'. A restaurant near our house employed a trolley with a huge tray, carrying about 15 items. The tray would then be slid on to the table easily to deliver food. It was incredibly efficient.

In many traditional Korean restaurants, we would sit on the floor and the dishes were served on a short table. This reminded us of our childhoods, when we did not have dining tables and sat on the floor to have our meals. In such restaurants, shoes are taken off and kept outside. At private residences too, footwear is taken off before entering. What caught my attention was that, more than once, when I took off my shoes and entered a restaurant, the staff would keep the shoes pointing outwards so that it was easy to slip them on while leaving.

In Korean restaurants, unlike most countries of the world, there is no custom of tipping. The rates mentioned in the menu card are inclusive of 10 per cent VAT. So, what you see on the menu card, you pay. There are no hidden costs.

Unlike in India where, if we went out in a group, we would order three or four dishes and share, in Korea, most of the time, people would order individual main courses and not share different items for variety. There would be common side dishes or a platter of sashimi to share, but the main course would be individual. Sudha's friend once insisted on ordering at least one item per person even if someone was not hungry, saying, 'They have been cooking since morning and have worked so hard, we must compensate them.' In a traditional restaurant, even after 10 dishes, the finale would be rice with soup or stew. There isn't a focus on dessert, at best, some fruit or a traditional Korean sweet like 'tteok', a type of rice cake, is served.

A question that non-Koreans often ask us is if Koreans really eat dogs. I was surprised to hear it the first time. I asked Korean colleagues whether it was true, and they smiled sheepishly, looked embarrassed and refused to either confirm or deny it. Once, Sudha and I went to a traditional market with Jay. As we entered, we saw dogs lined up in kennels and I remarked, 'What a nice arrangement to take care of dogs like a crèche when one is shopping.' Jay said softly, 'Those dogs are for sale. As meat.' I was shocked and kept quiet.

I later came to know that this practice of eating dogs is mostly a thing of the past and the Koreans don't like to talk about it, especially with foreigners. After a few years, I read in the newspapers about the administration's plan to discontinue the market where we had seen dogs for sale. Personally, I have never seen any restaurant serving, or any Korean eating, dog meat during my stay in Korea.

What we did come across were many Koreans who were extremely fond of their dogs. Most of them were small and furry, and it was interesting to see the dogs dressed up, especially in winters.

When it comes to food, Koreans, especially older people, prefer Korean food. Whenever I went out with my Korean colleagues, they would suggest a Korean restaurant and sometimes a Japanese one, since they knew I liked Japanese food. Sometimes, I would give them a treat in an Indian restaurant, which they enjoyed but found expensive.

Most Indian restaurants in Korea serve tandoori chicken, butter chicken, palak paneer, dal, naan, samosa and other such items. A thing most Koreans did not like was anything with coriander in it. With this limited exposure, Koreans felt all Indians eat this food. Of course, there were a few restaurants serving South Indian fare as well. I remember that one of our friends who managed the restaurant Ganga added dosa to his menu – he had two types of 'masala dosa', one stuffed with potato and one with chicken.

Sudha's friends were surprised when they came to our place and got to taste a wide variety of South Indian and Maharashtrian vegetarian food and, of course, everyone's favourite sev puri and chai.

The younger generation, especially women, seemed more adventurous and interested in trying out different cuisines. It was interesting to see McDonalds and KFC not so crowded, making them ideal dating spots for young couples.

The market for coffee is big in Korea. 'Dabangs' or cafes/ tea-and-coffee houses were popular in the second half of the twentieth century. They served various types of tea and coffee, and were places where one could socialize and even do business. In the twenty-first century, dabangs have given way to cafes and speciality stores, such as domestic and overseas brand franchises. Ediya Coffee leads in the domestic segment with over 3,000 outlets, and Starbucks is the star overseas brand with nearly 1,900 outlets – only lesser than the US and China, and almost equal to Japan but much higher in terms of per capita consumption. Within 100 m of our apartment there were three Starbucks outlets as well as many other cafes. It is said that an average Korean drinks two to three cups of coffee daily. The industry size is more than USD 12 billion, of which USD 10 billion is spent in cafes and restaurants.

We saw more women than men at the cafes. Coffee is not just a drink, it is an experience, and a café is also a place to hang out with friends. To be seen at a Starbucks perhaps adds to one's social stature as embracing of Western culture. Americano seemed to be the favourite order of my Korean friends, while I would go in for a cappuccino or a latte. One thing I did not get used to, even after six years, was having to specify 'hot coffee' while ordering in summer months because the default would be cold coffee. Luckily, seeing our Indian face, most of the times, the staff would ask, 'Hot or cold?'

In office, I would have green tea without milk and sugar. Then I came to know of a ready-mix coffee called Maxim that had milk and sugar, and just needed to be mixed with hot water. I liked the taste but avoided it because I could not have sugar. One day, a friend said to me, 'The sugar is at the bottom of the pack, if you hold tightly one inch from the bottom, the sugar will not go into your cup.' I tried it, and lo and behold! It was perfect coffee without sugar. I got hooked to it for the next few years and even brought it to India; Sudha's mother liked it very much.

Soju could be termed Korea's national alcoholic drink. It is a clear distilled spirit made from rice, wheat or barley with alcohol content ranging from 15 per cent to 50 per cent, and a price range from as low as USD 1 to much more in convenience stores. Soju constitutes about one-third of total alcoholic beverage sales in Korea. Whenever we had Korean food with friends and colleagues, drinking soju was mandatory during and after dinner. The taste is on the sweetish side, and I developed a liking for it from my very first sip. It is normally served cold and neat in a shot glass. It was common among my Korean friends to finish the drink in one shot, but I preferred to savour it. It was considered bad manners when everyone else was having it in one shot but I got away with it, being a senior in the group.

Makgeolli is a traditional Korean rice wine served in small bowls and has a milky, cloudy appearance like toddy in India. It is typically lower in alcohol content, about 5 to 8 per cent. Sudha liked makgeolli and would often have it with her Korean friends, especially on rainy days. I got an impression that makgeolli is a women's drink but then came to know that it is quite universal, is considered to have health benefits and goes well with certain dishes like pancakes.

'Maekju' (beer) is very popular and there are some Korean brands like Cass, Cloud and Hite that are doing great business. It is easily available in most convenience stores and in all restaurants. It is common practice to mix soju with beer, a concoction that is called 'so-maek'.

Sudha and I developed a taste for wine in Korea. It flowed in most formal events organized by corporate and government agencies. At times, champagne would be served as one entered, and for dinner there would be red and white wines paired with the courses, each served in appropriate glasses. This was a new learning experience for us. We were invited to join a wine club that organized wine parties at different locations including various Ambassadors' residences.

Among other alcoholic drinks, Koreans would have whisky but not so much vodka, gin or rum. Sometimes, at formal events where wine was served with dinner, a smaller group would go out separately and have whisky and soju. Whenever we went to our friend Shyam's Indian restaurant, especially with Indian friends, it was quite a sight to see the happy look on everyone's face after being able to order Old Monk rum in Korea, especially in winter.

In many countries, alcohol consumption in public places is a strict no. Not so in Korea. Once in a while, we enjoyed a can of beer in a park, by a stream or on a beach, and saw others doing it too. It was not rampant, though. We did not see anybody causing a nuisance or littering in a public place. I understand that since 2023, the administration has imposed restrictions on alcohol consumption in public places and fines are collected if one is seen drinking in no-alcohol areas.

Koreans are known to be heavy smokers. In my department, there were a few who would need a break every two-three hours for a smoke. What I appreciated was that everyone smoked in designated smoking areas, and not anywhere else. I guess this comes from discipline, and care and concern for others.

Hygiene and Jimjilbang

Interestingly, Koreans are so particular about their personal hygiene that they carry their toothbrushes and toothpastes with them at all times. In our office, it was a common sight to see employees brushing their teeth in the restroom after every meal. In fact, so prevalent is this hygiene habit that it is common practice to gift employees hampers with personal care products like toothpastes and soaps during festivals.

As in some developed countries, tap water is safe to drink in Korea.

Clean toilets are made available at every corner and in all public places. Restaurants undergo periodical inspection for hygiene standards among other parameters. We saw books and comics for children promoting hygiene and cleanliness by way of stories and pictures. Cleanliness inculcated at an early age becomes a habit. The Japanese are known to be paranoid about cleanliness; I must add, the Koreans are not far behind.

Koreans have a tradition of public baths called 'jimjilbang'. Historically, hot water was expensive to obtain individually and public baths were more cost-efficient because many could share the available hot water. Today, public baths are fewer in number than they were 50 years ago but are still a major attraction, where people do not see bathing as a task but as a way to relax and even socialize. It is common to see families spending quality time in a jimjilbang, or friends going together to have a good time. After a hard day's work, many people like to relax in sauna baths. I have heard stories from my colleagues that after late nights in office or a late-night party instead of going home, they have gone to a public bath to rest and come back to office the next day. Public baths are open all night in many places, and people do make the best of them at affordable prices.

Sudha once went for a sauna bath with her friends, but she enjoyed the chatting over soju and snacks much more than the actual bath. I did not venture to one, since I was not comfortable walking in the nude in the changing rooms. Koreans are very comfortable without clothes in the changing areas, be it public baths or changing rooms in swimming pools and golf courses.

There is lot of focus on public health and hygiene, and the slightest trace of pollution is taken very seriously. Every year, around spring time, the air pollution level goes up mainly due to the yellow dust that blows in from Mongolia and China into Korea. Air purifiers are commonly used at homes, offices and other establishments. There are apps to show pollution levels and alerts are sent on mobile phones if the level rises beyond a certain limit; then the masks come out. Koreans are very diligent in the use of masks as a precautionary measure, whether it is for pollution or while nursing a cold. This was a new experience for us – we never used masks in Korea anywhere until Covid-19.

Racism in Korea

In early 2024, a video went viral on social media in India that showed Indians being discriminated against in Korea. Many of our friends forwarded that video to us and wanted to know if it was true. This video may have been based on some bad experiences, but one cannot generalize based on stray incidents.

Fortunately, Sudha and I did not experience any discrimination during our six-year stay in Korea. We did come across clubs in Itaewon with boards that said, 'No foreigners please. Only Koreans.' Perhaps these clubs had had some bad experiences with foreigners. I remember walking with two Indian friends along a street once, both very senior executives in companies, and stopping by a fancy restaurant or club, simply looking at the menu on the board, when a bouncer came out and shouted, 'No over forty.' This club was only for youngsters under 40. We were surprised at this rude behaviour when we were not even thinking of going inside, but we moved on without thinking or discussing it too much.

What I have seen is that Koreans do not like the loud behaviour and bad manners of some foreigners, including

Indians. While shopping, if Indians or other foreigners try to bargain endlessly, Korean shopkeepers may get irritated because bargaining is not a common custom there. These kinds of biases can build up resentment over a period of time.

It is a fact that Koreans do look up to Westerners, especially white people. When it comes to others, they might have second thoughts or may not be as welcoming. Some may harbour a superiority complex vis-à-vis people from non-Western countries.

Spending a Virtue, Saving a Vice

As per conventional economic wisdom, you know a country is developed when citizens spend more and save less. At an individual level, Koreans spend a lot on skincare products, cosmetics and even cosmetic surgery. Brand-conscious citizens will spend a lot on expensive purses, bags, cosmetics and eating out.

Even when it comes to cars, Koreans prefer big sedans or sports utility vehicles (SUVs) over smaller cars. If they can afford it, the first choice is German cars like BMW, Mercedes and Audi. The market share for imported cars was 13 per cent in 2019. There are no three-wheelers and very few two-wheelers on the road. Two-wheelers are either used by delivery guys or bikers on their Harley Davidsons.

There are huge malls and thousands of shops in markets, streets and subway stations. One will not find people bargaining in big shops but perhaps they would on the streets or in small shops by saying 'kakkajusaeyo', which is a polite request for a discount. I knew only one Korean word when it came to shopping, 'olmaeyo', meaning 'how much'. I would not understand the response and ask them to write the amount on a calculator.

Something I observed in my circles in Korea was that there was constant comparison and wish to emulate others. One remark that rankled me was 'I am so jealous of you' or 'I envy you'. I heard this so many times from different people, both men and women. If you say that you are going to the US for a vacation, pat comes the comment, 'Oh, so nice. I envy you.' Or if one person says her child got admission to one of the top universities, the other will remark, 'Great, I am so jealous of you.' There is no malice in this remark, but it comes so spontaneously to Koreans as compared to Indians, who wouldn't say so as freely.

Koreans seem to be under pressure most of the time. Children's education puts pressure not only on the children but also on the parents. At work, there is the pressure of deadlines and to move up the hierarchy. In society, there is the pressure to look good and to not disobey or displease elders or bosses.

In spite of their higher incomes, Koreans are able to save much less than we do in India. While talking to my Korean friends, I found that they dreaded retirement, as they felt that they have not saved enough and might have to look for work even after they retire. Being a developed economy, the interest earned on their savings is too low to take care of post-retirement life, though medical needs are taken care of by the government and free public transport is provided after 65.

I found it amusing when my colleagues would ask me, 'What will you do after retirement? How will you manage without working?' I would tell them that I had some savings, and that the interest rates in India were better than in developed countries and that it should be good enough for a decent lifestyle. They could not believe it. Sudha would jokingly tell her friends that we can always fall back on our son's support if need be, and her friends would be aghast at the thought of depending on children in old age.

Affluence also brings with it wastage. I found that people from the older generations, who may have seen difficult times, were careful not to waste anything. Our CEO, a senior citizen, once told younger people not to leave anything on their plates – recounting how difficult it was to get food in his childhood. I could relate to this; even in India, we see this trend of wasting food with the neo-rich or younger generations.

In the office, I had the habit of taking a print on both sides of the paper, and tried to influence others to do the same. It took a long time to convince people to print on both sides. Only a few from my team started doing it and that too only for me, and not if the printout was meant for others.

We Indians are so used to a frugal mindset, trying to save at every opportunity or reuse or recycle things, whereas Koreans would prefer to go for a new one believing that buying more and consuming more would be good for the economy. I remember studying John Keynes in college who famously said, 'Spending is a virtue, saving is a vice.' The Koreans, it seems, have really taken Keynes seriously!

Housing, especially in urban areas, and education are the two biggest expenses for a family. Buying a house outright could be very costly, in which case one may opt for a rented place. There is a third option, that was new to me, since I had not seen it in India. One could pay a hefty deposit, almost 60 to 80 per cent of the market value of the house, pay zero rent, and then get the deposit back at the end of the lease period. The company opted for this option which is called 'jeonse' in Korean. We stayed in an apartment with such an arrangement throughout our time in Korea.

Education in Korean schools is not so expensive. But the coaching classes (hagwon) that children go to can be quite pricey. International schools are exorbitant. Due to these high costs and commitments, we came across many instances where the young generation got married very late or did not want to marry at all.

Weddings and Funerals

Sudha tried more than once to fix a match for her friend's daughters, but in vain. In one case, there was a difference in religion, Buddhist and Christian, which was not acceptable to Sudha's friend. In another case, the boy was the eldest in the family and was hence rejected. This was because in Korea the eldest son and his wife have more responsibility during Chuseok, where one prays and offers food to ancestors.

While Sudha tried to fix a match, she did not get to attend any weddings during our stay in Korea. I got the opportunity to do so twice. Both were Christian-style weddings in a hotel – well-organized events with a formal sit-down lunch or dinner along with wine. It is customary to give cash gifts in an envelope, and there would be someone from the family at the entrance who would receive the envelope and record it in a register with the name of the guest. Some people also send huge bouquets of flowers, which are displayed at the entrance.

Funerals are given a lot of importance, and people make it a point to attend the funerals or to at least pay a condolence visit. When one of our colleagues lost his aged mother, we went to the hospital, where they had funeral halls with catering service to serve traditional Korean meals along with soju to people visiting the family members of the deceased. One normally gives an envelope of cash at the entrance, then offers condolence to the family members, pays respect to the departed soul's portrait and then proceeds to the meal. This visiting is usually done on the first or second day, and on the third day the coffin is taken to the cemetery. I was told that more and more people were opting for cremation nowadays rather than for burial.

At SsangYong, if an employee belonging to a distant town or village lost a parent or other family members, buses would be arranged for the employee's colleagues to attend the funeral or to visit the employee's family to offer condolences and hand over an envelope of cash. When Sudha returned from India after attending her mother's funeral in 2019, her Korean friends came to our place to offer their condolences along with an envelope of cash.

Since accepting cash was not our custom, Sudha had to politely decline to her friends' surprise.

Demographic Challenges

With an increasing number of young people in Korea delaying getting married or not marrying at all, and with death rates now exceeding birth rates, the natural growth rate of the population is in the negative. Korea is facing demographic challenges with an aged population.

In rural areas, it is difficult to get farm labour. There are many cases where Koreans in villages and small towns marry belonging to from poor families from countries like the Philippines, Thailand and Vietnam. Even in Seoul, Sudha had friends in her advanced Korean class who had come from these countries after marrying Koreans working as bus drivers, house-keeping and maintenance staff for a better lifestyle. These girls would share their domestic problems with Sudha and she would counsel them. In most cases, the bone of contention would be cultural differences and in-laws' expectations. Sudha would advise them to adjust to the new realities, as they had come to Korea to lead a more comfortable life.

In urban areas, we were surprised to see some young Korean girls marry middle-aged well-to-do Westerners. My Indian friend used to joke that among the senior leadership team in his office, he was the only one who had not married a Korean girl; many of his colleagues from the US and Europe had young Korean wives.

Koreans, with a sense of national pride and great discipline, have worked hard and with their strong commitment, have taken their country to great heights. While development brings prosperity, it also poses new challenges. Issues like low fertility rates, an aged population, inequality of class and gender, and the continuing close nexus between business and politics pose a challenge to society's evolution. After having understood briefly the journey of the country and the countrymen, let me now share my experience in the corporate world in Korea.

4
Work–Life Imbalance?

I still remember vividly the day in December 2012 when I was summoned by my big boss while working with Mahindra & Mahindra in Mumbai.

Big boss: Our current CFO is completing two years in Korea, and will be moving to a new role. Will you go to Korea as CFO of SsangYong Motor Company?

I replied: Yes, I am ready to go to Korea.

There was absolutely no hesitation on my part, neither did I say that I will discuss it with my family.

It was as if I was waiting for this offer. I had already discussed it with Sudha – that I would accept any good global assignment that came my way – and she had agreed to stop all her activities and move with me if required. Our son had shifted with his wife and son to Florence, Italy, and we had no responsibilities back home.

I was told that our Korean CEO would like to see me when he came to India next, and only then would my Korea assignment be confirmed.

A couple of months later, in February 2013, I met the Korean CEO in Mumbai, and we had a good conversation. Something he said gave me an insight into Korean thinking on gender roles and his expectations from a CFO.

He said, 'The CEO is like the man of the house, going out to meet clients and to get business. The CFO is like the homemaker, looking after the finances and well-being of the company.'

After our 'look-and-see' visit to Korea in March 2013, and after receiving the CEO's approval, it was time to prepare to depart. Though, I still had a few months to see through the March year-end accounts and audit in Mumbai.

As we approached June end, the excitement of going to an unknown place started dawning on us, and after the farewell parties, I realized that this may be the last of farewells, and that I may retire after my Korea stint.

We had already finalized our house and basic furniture in Seoul, so when we reached there with four suitcases and two handbags on 6 July 2013, we settled in in a few hours and started entertaining colleagues at home from the very next day.

My First Day at SsangYong Motor Company

I joined SsangYong Motor Company as CFO on 8 July 2013 after Mahindra & Mahindra acquired the company in 2011.

I reached office at 8 a.m. since I was told all senior executives have to come half an hour before office time. The weekly Monday morning meeting of executives chaired by the CEO started at 8.30 a.m. and lasted till 9.45 a.m. I then had a short meeting with the CEO.

At 10 a.m., I was taken to the labour union president's office, along with my interpreter. I was told that protocol demanded that I meet the CEO and the labour union president before I start my day.

After the usual greetings in Korean and English through our interpreter, the first question he asked me was, 'Where do you stay?'

I replied, 'Bundang.'

Later, I came to know that where I lived was a suburb, which was considered modern but not as posh as expensive downtown areas like Gangnam or Yongsan. To give examples from Mumbai, Bundang was similar to Bandra, while Gangnam and Yongsan were like Peddar Road or Malabar Hill.

The next question was, 'How big is your house?'

I was taken aback for a moment. Then I replied, 'This is my first day in your country. I don't know what you term as a big or small house. All I can say is that it is a comfortable place for me and my wife.'

Fortunately, he did not have a follow-up question and left it at that. Then he said that being a Mahindra representative, I should convince Mahindra & Mahindra to invest more and help the company. I replied that I was now a SsangYong employee and together we should ensure that we didn't have to ask for any funding from the parent company.

This meeting with the labour union president prepared me for future interactions with the labour union.

I returned to my office and was handed my identity card, laptop and mobile. In short, I was ready to get started. Since my predecessor was still vacating the office, I was asked to sit in another cabin. I had seen cabinets with a lot of files in his office in the morning.

When I moved to that office the next day, all the files were gone. I had heard about Korean efficiency, and this was my first experience of it. I was supposed to start from scratch. I asked for the files to be brought back and after review, retained more than 70 per cent of them since they were about budgets and board meeting presentations.

It was going to be a busy week with wage negotiation meetings, review meetings and preparation for the quarterly board meeting. I had studied the previous quarter's board presentation and the budget-working before reaching Seoul, and hence was able to hit the ground running.

Mahindra's Tryst with SsangYong

SsangYong Motor Company was an old automobile company specializing in sports utility vehicles (SUVs) that had gone bankrupt. Mahindra & Mahindra had acquired control of it after a successful bid in an auction at the end of 2010.

SsangYong was started in the 1960s and had undergone several ownership changes. The conglomerate SsangYong Group acquired this company in 1986 and retained it till the company went bankrupt during the Asian financial crisis in 1997. Later, SAIC Motor Corp., a Chinese company, acquired SsangYong and, after five years, walked out during the 2008 financial crisis. There were allegations in the Korean media that the Chinese company acquired SsangYong only to get access to its technology. The term I read in the newspapers for this was 'eat and run'. When the company was under court receivership in 2009, a major restructuring of workforce was planned, which led to a violent strike.

When Mahindra & Mahindra successfully bid and acquired over 70 per cent stake in SsangYong, the first challenge, besides turning it around, was to inspire confidence among employees, suppliers, customers, the general public and the Korean media that Mahindra & Mahindra was here to stay and not to 'eat and run'.

It was a good acquisition for Mahindra & Mahindra, as SsangYong was ideal for its automotive business growth. Both were specialists in SUVs. The benefits envisaged were joint-vehicle and engine-platform development, joint sourcing (which could give benefits of scale) and leveraging the global distribution network to increase exports for both companies.

Mahindra & Mahindra decided to have a Korean CEO and an Indian CFO, along with six other Mahindra expats in functions like product planning, sourcing, exports, manufacturing engineering and human resources, to be the link between SsangYong and Mahindra & Mahindra to facilitate synergy.

Coming out of bankruptcy is never easy. Confidence is low all around, be it with customers, suppliers, bankers or employees. Why would a customer take a risk and buy a SsangYong vehicle with little assurance of the service that may be required for more than 10 years? Why would good senior executives join SsangYong when its future was uncertain?

These were the challenges the company had to grapple with as it began its task of normalizing operations and building confidence among stakeholders. The company had a good range of SUVs, and managed to get some senior executives from Hyundai, Kia and other companies.

In the automobile industry, a new vehicle platform needs at least four years of development time and an investment of more than USD 200 million. The company made some quick facelift changes to existing vehicles and, with good marketing, brought some excitement in the market to win back customers. Sales in the domestic market started to increase and exports started doing well, especially those to Russia.

When I joined SsangYong in 2013, we had achieved 60 per cent capacity utilization; more than half the production was for export sales. We managed to break-even that year. It was a remarkable achievement, considering that Mahindra & Mahindra had planned to achieve break-even after three years but had managed to advance it by one year. Confidence was back among employees as well as among customers and suppliers.

However, two adverse developments in 2014 pushed the company back in the red. The Supreme Court of Korea gave a verdict to include certain allowances in the calculation of overtime and retirement benefits. This

First experience of cherry blossoms at Jinhae

Enjoying the fall colours at Nami Island

A view of the factory's vehicle stock during snowfall

Seoul – Development on both sides of the Han River

Buddha temple at Busan

Volcanic columnar rocks at Jeju

Cheonggyecheon stream

Walking track along the stream near our house

Starfield Library

Hanok (traditional house) and pots to preserve kimchi for the year

Sudha's friends Helena (centre) and Christine at the egg art exhibition

Outside Gyeongbokgung Palace in a hanbok (traditional Korean dress)

Pajeon (pancake) with a variety of side dishes

Savouring our favourite Dak-galbi (chicken BBQ) with family and our driver Jay

Lunch with Korean friends

In police volunteer jacket

Live telecast of Sudha singing the police anthem on the 74th Korea Police National Day

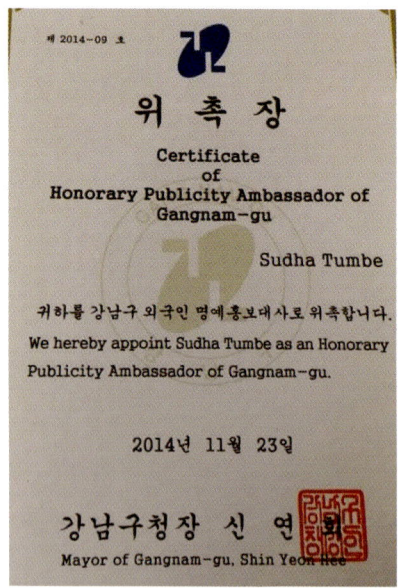

Gangnam Publicity Ambassador certificate

Playing golf with colleagues and a banker

Friends wearing Indian clothes, including sarees, at ICCK Diwali Ball

With international friends from Bundang – 'Bundangos'

Anand Mahindra and seniors at the G4 Rexton launch in Seoul

ICCK team with PM Narendra Modi

With Indian friends at our farewell party

increased the employee cost for the company by more than USD 50 million per annum.

Additionally, Russia annexed Crimea, which resulted in the value of the Russian ruble plummeting, adversely impacting exports to Russia and Ukraine. Since half of SsangYong's exports were to these regions, sales and profitability were significantly impacted.

The year 2015 saw the launch of a new vehicle, Tivoli, which captured the hearts of many Koreans, especially the younger generation. This was the first project approved (in early 2011) after Mahindra's acquisition, and the CEO had committed to launch this vehicle in January 2015, which he did. This gave us a glimpse of the commitment that Koreans show to whatever task they take on hand and their excellence in project management – be it timeline, cost or quality. Thanks to the success of Tivoli, 2016 was the only year when SsangYong made a profit.

The automobile business involves huge capital expenditure to roll out new products every year, and to meet mandatory emission and safety norms. And this can happen through scale when the company grows sales numbers and revenue/profits. It is significant to mention that, as per the plan, SsangYong launched new products every year from 2015 to 2019. Domestic sales and market share in Korea grew year-on-year as per the plan. SsangYong was third, behind Hyundai and Kia, but ahead of General Motors and Renault Samsung in the domestic market. Unfortunately, total sales remained stagnant throughout these years. New products did reasonably well, but existing products' sales continued to slide as export markets shrank and competition intensified in Korea as well as in the export markets.

How did the company manage to invest over USD 200 million every year in spite of losses? Fortunately, the company was making cash profits and, with some loans, was able to fund the investment required for new products. Mahindra & Mahindra's reputation helped to obtain loans from foreign banks. But this could not be sustained with 60 per cent capacity utilization and static revenues of around USD 3 billion. SsangYong continued to struggle financially in view of the increase in employee cost due to the Supreme Court verdict and the loss of Russian market that made a huge dent on export sales.

The benefits envisaged at the time of acquisition were slow to materialize due to cultural differences and an initial lack of confidence.

There were some benefits in joint sourcing by way of cost-savings, but not to the full potential. Koreans focus so much on quality that they are apprehensive about sourcing from countries like India, China and Thailand simply to reduce cost. And if the vehicle sales are stagnant, there is very little scope to get benefit of scale.

Joint development of products was attempted between SsangYong's and Mahindra's engineers and achieved to a small extent. Initially, there was lot of apprehension on the part of the Koreans and they kept citing government regulations for not sharing data or technology, and sometimes the labour union took objection. Mahindra & Mahindra was also careful lest there be a misunderstanding that the Indians, like the Chinese, were only interested in taking technology. The cultural differences and different product requirements for various markets made the task of a common product platform development very difficult. Mahindra did develop a common engine and the XUV 300 vehicle in India using the Tivoli platform, after paying a fee for SsangYong technology and modifying the vehicle for the Indian market.

SsangYong exported mostly to developed countries in Europe, and Mahindra exported mainly to developing countries in Asia, Africa, South America and Europe. The result was that SsangYong products were too expensive for emerging markets and Mahindra products had limited demand in developed markets. Rexton from the SsangYong stable was introduced in India in the high-end SUV segment. However, after showing initial promise, it did not do too well. Other SsangYong products overlapped with Mahindra's & Mahindra portfolio for the Indian market.

Korea was known for advanced automobile technology, thanks to Hyundai and Kia. So, it was natural for SsangYong employees to assume that they had an upper hand while dealing with Indian engineers. Sometimes, language and clear communication were an issue. This was evident in many instances, and I felt that the Koreans would have preferred a Korean company to own SsangYong rather than an Indian company. The following example might reiterate my feelings about this. Mahindra's finance arm, Mahindra Financial Services, was in talks for nearly two years with a Korean financial institution to start a finance company in Korea in order to finance automobile sales. When things did not work out, Mahindra Financial Services decided not to go ahead with the project. Within four or five months, SsangYong finalized a similar deal with a local financial institution, and the finance company was formed. I was amazed at the speed at which all this happened.

I was surprised to observe how Koreans, who earn foreign exchange on exports and own companies outside Korea, do not like it when foreign companies make money in Korea and want to pay dividend to their parent companies. When SsangYong made a small profit, there were some discussions about possible dividends in future, and I could sense the discomfort among my Korean colleagues. An Indian friend, who was the CEO in another company, validated my observation by saying that every time they planned to pay dividends, there would be an objection from the labour union.

In the second half of 2019, the company started to incur cash losses when a new product launched earlier in the year did not do as well as expected and sales started slowing down. More cash was required to fund the operations and capital expenditure by way of new loans. The banks insisted that the parent company also invest an equal amount to match the loan. This was during the time when there was a lockdown in end March 2020 due to Covid-19 and uncertainty prevailed.

In this scenario, the Mahindra & Mahindra board decided that it would not be prudent to invest further in SsangYong. Mahindra & Mahindra tried to get an investor, but due to the global slowdown precipitated by the pandemic, it did not work out. Finally, after one year, SsangYong had to file for bankruptcy. And more than a year after this, SsangYong got a new Korean owner. Today, it has a new name – KG Mobility Company.

Mahindra & Mahindra owned and managed SsangYong for 10 years and tried its best to turn around the company. New products were introduced every year with substantial investment, labour issues were resolved amicably and goodwill was earned in Korean society. When Mahindra & Mahindra decided not to invest further, employees, media and the general public understood its position and did not accuse them of an 'eat and run' policy. For Mahindra & Mahindra, it was a great learning experience to manage a large overseas listed company, and also to gain exposure to global best practices through an exchange of ideas in product development, sourcing, manufacturing systems and selling in global markets.

Now let me come back to my personal experience in the company. My team members were comfortable in their language, all the meetings were in Korean except for the board meetings. For internal meetings, my interpreter would translate in English for us expats, and at board meetings she would translate in Korean for my colleagues. I soon realized the importance of my interpreter and depended a lot on her skills. And I must say, she was very good at it, having lived earlier in Germany and China.

I had come from Mumbai where I would be busy all the time following up on phone and emails, attending meetings, and had very little time for myself. And here, in Korea, I suddenly found myself with lot of 'free' time on hand. The reason was that because of language being an issue, initially, there were hardly any phone calls and emails.

Koreans respect hierarchy so much that they would not bring anything to me unless it was absolutely essential and ready to report. So, I gradually got used to this newfound 'freedom' from routine activities, and started reading and analysing global businesses and labour-related issues, while also strategizing for future.

Language and Numbers

During my time in Korea, I could not learn the language, except for a few words and numbers. However, Sudha was fluent both in written and spoken Korean. I had the privilege of having an interpreter in office and an English-speaking driver who was of great help outside office. Learning the Korean numbers was important because I realized that most Koreans used to get confused while expressing numbers in million or billion. This is because they think in Korean, which has different units, i.e., ten thousand and hundred million like we have lakh and crore in India. To make matters worse, my team had to report to the parent company in India by speaking in lakhs and crores of rupees. Fortunately, although the units are different in Korean, one writes the numbers in English.

I called my team one day and explained to them how to remember these different units. I said, 'Up to three 0s is no problem – 1,000 is common to India, Korea and the rest of the world. Four 0s (10,000) is Korean "maan", five 0s is Indian lakh, six 0s is million, seven 0s is Indian crore, eight 0s is Korean "eog", nine 0s is billion.' I am glad to say that my team got it right and never made a mistake while reporting to Mahindra & Mahindra, India.

The Korean currency is won (KRW). When we reached Korea in 2013, USD 1 was equivalent to about KRW 1,000 -1,100. So, to make it easy for foreigners to understand, Koreans and even shop keepers would say USD 10 instead of KRW 10,000 (*Maan* Won). In 2024, the equation has changed: USD 1 is close to KRW 1,400. Similarly, a KRW 10,000 currency note was equivalent to INR 500 (600 today), and that's how we remembered and converted. In fact, this equation has come so handy that we have shared it with so many Indian visitors who struggled with currency conversion initially.

It took time to get used to everything being translated by my interpreter. Initially, when I asked a question in English to my team members, my interpreter would translate my question, my team members would discuss among themselves and then my interpreter would again translate for me. The first one or two times, the time gap was so much that I forgot what I had asked in the first place. I decided that I should note down my question to ensure I got the right response.

If I gave any instruction over the telephone to those of my colleagues who understood English, they would get very uncomfortable and would request me to send an email so that they could translate or come to my office to speak with my interpreter. Gradually, things improved, as my team members also worked hard on their English. As CFO, I had to approve huge amounts for which I depended heavily on my interpreter. Teams from various departments came to me and my interpreter with a lot of back-up material, all in Korean, to justify the proposals, and I realized I was approving these big amounts based only on what I understood from my interpreter.

Many of my Korean colleagues spoke only in Korean. At times, my interpreter would not be around. Some of my colleagues could speak English, though they were not very confident. What would upset me was when they would joke and laugh when I was sitting with them and I could not understand a word. They would not bother to explain or summarize what was said, even when I asked them to. I would term this as bad manners in India when my teammates spoke in Marathi when a non-Marathi person was in the group and would correct them. But I could not do that in Korea and gave up after some attempts.

In SsangYong, employees were encouraged to learn English. One of the parameters for performance appraisal of managers was their English test score. I found many employees got good scores in written English but were shy to actually speak the language.

I am reminded of some interesting incidents as to how language and culture can lead to misunderstandings. Once, our Indian boss was not happy with a proposal for a new project and in frustration said, 'Do what you want.' When I saw the draft of the minutes of the meeting, it said that the boss cleared the proposal and had asked us to do it as proposed. That was the literal interpretation of 'do what you want'. Of course, this was later corrected.

In another case, when our Indian boss indicated that a certain person had been identified to be transferred to Korea, if and when required, it was taken as an instruction, and a cabin with a name plate was kept ready within two days, only to be removed later.

When a capex proposal for a huge amount was presented, our Indian boss did not want to discourage the team by rejecting it outright and hence said, 'We will see later.' After the meeting, the project leader came out and declared that the project had been approved and to start work on it. We realized that if one does not say a clear 'no', it was assumed to be 'yes'.

During a budget meeting in the initial years, our Indian boss asked the sales team whether they could increase the sales numbers in the budget by 5 per cent. The sales team agreed immediately, to our surprise. In India, I have seen how the sales team would try and convince the CEO that they had already stretched the numbers and could not increase them anymore. Or they would reluctantly agree to a small increase of less than 1 per cent. But there were more surprises in store!

When we worked out the financials with 5 per cent more sales numbers, the bottom line did not improve but worsened. The sales team explained that to sell more vehicles, they would have to spend much more on sales incentives and marketing, resulting in worsening the financials. We went back to the original sales numbers and learnt an important lesson. In Korean, 'ne' means yes and 'aneyo' means no. We used to joke that the 'naysayers' become 'yes-men' in Korea.

While in Korea, it dawned on me for the first time how bad I was at Indian languages because when I spoke in Hindi or Marathi, every sentence included a few English words. Not so with Koreans. They do not use a single English word when they speak, making it very difficult to eavesdrop! When we Mahindra & Mahindra colleagues conversed in Hindi and did not want others to understand, we started speaking slowly and tried to use only Hindi words. I must say, our Hindi improved as a result!

I learnt a few Korean words, but not sentences, which I used occasionally to convey things when there was nobody to help me. In my apartment complex, our security guard without fail greeted me daily with 'annyeonghaseyo' and I responded in Hindi, 'Kaise ho' (how are you), which sounded similar to 'haseyo', and he used to bow and acknowledge it.

I was surprised to note that, many times, Koreans did not understand my English. They have learnt American English and perhaps found the Queen's English or my accent different. One thing with which I had the most trouble was, 'Where do you stay?' They would just not get it. Then I would try, 'Where do you live?' If still I did not get an answer, I would try, 'Where is your house?' Similarly, if we had to ask 'where is the toilet?' many times we would not get any response. Then we would say 'where is the restroom?', 'where is the washroom?' or 'where is the bathroom?' and we would get a response, 'Oh! Hwajangsil!' We realized then that there are so many words for the word 'toilet' in English, but we must remember the Korean word for it. This was in the initial stages, before we realized there were toilets at every corner in Korea with clear signboards.

One thing I missed in Korea was humour in office. In India, I was used to some jokes with colleagues to ease the work pressure. But here, seniors were supposed to be serious. Besides, subtle play of English words that I enjoyed might not be understood. As per Sudha's suggestion, I decided to check whether my interpreter, whose English was good, understood my humour. One day, I told her, 'I had been to a training programme in India where I learnt how to improve my listening skills. After that, I did not speak to Sudha for a week.' She asked, 'Did you quarrel with her?' I said, 'No, I did not want to interrupt her.' She did not get the joke and asked me, 'Why?' That day I realized that I should continue to be serious in office.

After a year, I was practising a speech in my office when my interpreter barged in and said, 'You are talking to yourself!' In mock seriousness, I said, 'Yes, I do that sometimes when I need expert advice.' This time, she got the joke and burst out laughing.

What's in a Name?

How does one remember names in a non-English speaking country? It is very difficult. I realized that it may be the same for Koreans and other foreigners to remember tongue-twisting Indian names like Sivaramkrishnan. For that matter, it may be difficult to know whether the person is male or a female by simply reading their name. How will a Korean know whether Radha is female and Krishna is male? Similarly, even after more than six years in Korea, I must admit that I will not be able to say confidently whether the person is male or female just from the name.

One thing I observed with most Korean names, and something that is different from Indian names, is that the Korean ones are short. For example, Park Yeon-sik, Kim Ji-young. Normally, the surname comes first while addressing a person. Some of the most common family names in Korea are Kim, Park, Lee, Chung, Choi, Song and Kang. In Korean, some alphabets are interchangeable like P and B, K and G, R and L. So, 'Gangnam' can be 'Kangnam' and 'Busan' can be 'Pusan', but 'POSCO' (the steel company) is not 'BOSCO'. 'Lee' is written and pronounced in Korean as 'ee'. As R sounds like L, our colleague 'Rao' was called 'Lao' and 'root cause' sounded like 'loot cause'.

Some of the Koreans adopted English names, like Helen, Herbert and so on, when they interacted with foreigners. One of my friends whose name was Hwi-jae used to get introduced to Indians as Vijay, which sounds like Hwi-jae. In Korea, women do not change their last names after marriage, and children take the father's last name. Just like we add the suffix 'ji' in Hindi to address someone respectfully, Koreans will add 'ssi' or 'nim', say 'Sudha-ssi' or 'Vasudev-nim'.

I used to remember family names like Park, Lee and so on with initials or designations. I remember my Friday meetings with our finance company executives, where I was surrounded by no less than five Parks. The CEO and CFO of the finance company, my treasury and management control department heads, and my interpreter all had the family name Park. While I could address my interpreter as 'Ms Park', I had to remember the full name of the other Parks. I can say that it was no walk in the park.

Once, one of our Indian colleagues had brought some snacks to celebrate Diwali. He said in Hindi that the 'chuklee' was sent by his wife Maithilee on the occasion of 'Diwalee'. We were worried whether our boss Mr Lee heard him and thought we are talking about him, especially because of the word 'Chuck Lee'!

Work Ethic

The best part of my work life was that everything was well planned and there was very little uncertainty. In India, there would be times when I would struggle with uncertainty due to industry practices, which was not the case in Korea.

For instance, in India, more than 70 per cent of the billing and collection of money would happen in the last few days of the month, and payments to suppliers had to be made daily, leading to uncertainty of cash flows. In Korea, collection was more or less even throughout the month, with about 30 per cent happening in the last five days, and payment to suppliers was mostly done on the last day of the month. So, were certain about the cash position at any point of time.

In India, there was a practice of negotiating with suppliers for price changes, and settling as late as possible by giving retrospective amendments to the purchase orders. This made cost and profit estimations very difficult. In Korea, the practice of retrospective price amendments was rare, which made our life easy.

When it came to VAT refunds from the government, in India, we would have to follow up for years and deal with the not-so-cooperative government assessment officers to get back our own money. In Korea, we got our VAT refunds seamlessly in every quarter without any follow-ups.

In Korea, meetings were few, and they started and ended on time. The presentations were exhaustive, with a lot of back up data to address queries. These were circulated to attendees in advance so that they could come well prepared for the meeting. I observed that, unlike at Mahindra & Mahindra – where employees freely voiced their opinion in a meeting – in SsangYong, even if a person knew the subject, they would only speak when asked to. This came from the Korean respect for hierarchy and others' time. As a result, I found that meetings were shorter and to the point, and decision-making was faster. For my board meetings, the presentation was readied five days in advance, and I had enough time to prepare and attend dinner meetings before it. This was in contrast to India, where I would be busy going through the presentation till the night before.

Koreans are known to be hard working. Typically, in SsangYong, officers and managers work for 10 to 12 hours daily, and sometimes even on Saturdays. The weekends were off, but production departments would work overtime depending on the demand. Historically and culturally, Koreans have worked hard; taking leave is frowned upon. Old-timers did not believe in taking leave for recreation. This tradition continues in companies like SsangYong, where most employees took very few leaves and preferred to encash them once a year.

As per general practice in Korea, most employees had three meals at the workplace, viz., breakfast, lunch at noon and dinner at 6 p.m., after which some would continue their work. Sudha's friends used the term 'three-meal-husband' and complained that after retirement, their husbands would be at home and expect them to cook.

In our company, several hundred employees stayed in a dormitory at the factory to avoid long-distance commutes after working late shifts. They were called 'weekend husbands'. Some of my friends who were weekend husbands used to jokingly tell me how busy their weekends were with all the household chores that piled up for them over the week.

I was told before going to Korea that one has to be very strict at the time of budgeting because, once the budget is approved, people tend to spend and there was very little incentive to save, unlike in India. I found that while for Koreans, quality, time and then cost is priority, for Indians, it is always cost that is the first priority. As a result, Indians would try to save costs at every stage, and in the bargain, it could impact quality and completion time.

I found Koreans to be dedicated, disciplined and process-oriented. This ensured execution excellence. In SsangYong, a full-fledged training centre, including accommodation facilities, a cafeteria and a recreation centre, was completed in six months – as promised at the project approval stage. Give a task to a Korean and rest assured that it will be done on time, and without any follow-ups too. I experienced this in my early days. My team members did not like it when I followed up to check if work was on track. 'Why are you asking? It will be done, don't worry,' they would say. The buzz word in Korean is 'palli, palli', which means to do or act fast, an equivalent of the Hindi 'jaldi, jaldi'.

Commitment to tasks is a given. I remember an instance when I had to make a presentation at 8.30 a.m. and had called my colleague to show me the presentation half an hour earlier. He promptly did so. In the afternoon, after the meeting was over, he asked me if he could leave early. I asked him the reason. It had so happened that while coming to office in the morning, his car had met with an accident and had been badly damaged. Yet, he was in office on time, before 8 a.m., and now wanted to go early to complete the car insurance formalities. There was no indication of his ordeal when he took me through the presentation in the morning. I was awestruck by his commitment.

Importance of Hierarchy

Historically, Korean society has been hierarchical, and the military training accentuates this. When you meet a person for the first time, it is customary to exchange business cards. The angle of bowing down will depend upon the designation. If a person is vice president or president, and the other person is a junior, the junior will bow that much more and give the other person utmost respect.

The significance of hierarchy in Korea manifests in many ways in office, at home, everywhere. In office, seniors are supposed to do the thinking and set direction for others to execute. Once an instruction is given, it will be done on time. The flip side is that innovation becomes difficult in the big corporations, since younger employees hesitate to give ideas to their seniors. I remember, initially, I used to call for brainstorming sessions with my team like we used to do in India, but then gave up. I realized that junior members were not forthcoming in giving ideas but expected direction from seniors.

In office, people are addressed with their designations as suffixes, like manager ('gwajang'), deputy general manager ('chajang'), general manager ('bujang'), director ('sangmu'), vice president ('busajang') and president ('sajang'). There is role clarity at all levels. The role of the team leader is very important. They act as a bridge between those who do the work and the seniors who set direction.

In formal meetings, a lot of importance is given to the seating arrangement. For example, in labour management meetings, the labour union president would sit opposite the CEO, the labour union vice president opposite a vice president, and so on. Once, our CEO was not available for a meeting with the labour union, so our vice president of manufacturing, was to preside over the meeting. The labour union president excused himself and requested his vice president to lead the discussions. Even for a new product launch, which is mainly a marketing event, in our company, the labour union president accompanied the CEO most of the time.

On my first day in office, I was surprised to see my huge cabin, almost four times the size of what I had in India. When I asked a colleague why we had such big cabins, his response was, 'To intimidate the visitor. An aura is created around the senior-most executives and people should be scared or respectful. They should realize they are meeting an important person.' One of our CEOs used to be very serious in office, so much so that people would be scared of him. I never saw him smile while in office. But after office, during our dinner meetings, he would be very friendly, speak freely and would even laugh.

In India, if our CEO was to attend a suppliers' or dealers' conference, he would sit through all the presentations. However, in Korea, the CEO will walk in only in the last hour and go straight to the stage to give his speech and present the awards. Thereafter, he would be present at dinner and interact with the guests.

An Indian friend of mine who served as the CFO of a company, shared interesting insights on this topic. While Koreans respect hierarchy and will obey orders, he felt that in some cases his colleagues did not share information, since he was a foreigner. He felt their loyalties were primarily to fellow Koreans even though they were supposed to report to him. I did not experience this first-hand and if any information was withheld from me, I was not aware of it.

HR Practices in SsangYong

Being an old company, SsangYong's HR practices were a bit old-fashioned, and gradually Mahindra & Mahindra's HR practices and performance management systems were put in place. For example, at SsangYong, promotions at deputy general manager (DGM) or general manager (GM) levels used to come after four to five years, and were typically based on seniority rather than merit. Over a long period, with low attrition levels, there were more DGMs and GMs than junior employees, which skewed the structure and made employees at all levels unhappy. Employees up to manager level had the protection of the labour union. At the executive/director level, there were one-year contracts that brought about uncertainty and insecurity in the minds of senior employees, and a tendency to take decisions for the short term developed.

I also witnessed strong consequence management, especially at the executive/director level, where employees were asked to leave for non-performance. Since the rewards for success were not much but punishment for failure was severe, there was a natural tendency to play safe and not take risks. At lower levels like GM or below, it was not surprising to see a person demoted and asked to report to his junior, who got promoted in the same department, from the next day. What I found more surprising was that the demoted senior would behave as if nothing had happened, at least outwardly, and the show would go on. I was told of some instances in other companies where a person, after being dismissed, continued to leave home daily and return late evening as if he were working, so that neighbours, and sometimes even family members, did not know that he had lost his job.

One glaring difference I observed between SsangYong and Mahindra & Mahindra was the recruitment process. Vacancies and manpower requirements across departments were consolidated, discussed and approved by senior management, like we did in India. Thereafter, interviews were arranged over one or two weeks for all the positions. The interview panel included the CEO, CFO, HR director and the concerned department director. What surprised me was that even for junior, entry-level positions, this senior management panel was involved in the recruitment process, unlike in Mahindra & Mahindra, where HR managers and department heads completed the recruitment process. Only for the recruitment in very senior positions were the CEO, CFO and senior management involved in India.

At SsangYong, four to five candidates were interviewed simultaneously. It was quite a sight to see the way young people that walked in for an interview. It was obvious that the young men were back from their military training – their gait and posture indicated so. They would sit straight, hands on their thighs, serious faces, ready for a barrage of questions. The interview being in Korean and with my interpreter not accompanying me, I could not understand a word. My role was to test the candidates' English language skills. Also, Koreans emphasize recruiting freshers because they think that the freshers can be moulded into the company's loyal soldiers.

In the finance and accounts department, I was surprised to note that there was not a single professionally qualified accountant, like a CA or CPA. This was a unique practice of not hiring into the company but seeking help from consultants when required, as it turned out to be a much cheaper option. But I must say that my team of accountants and the finance team were very competent, having worked in the company for a long time.

There was a system where we hired one of the Big Four accounting firms, like KPMG or E&Y, on retainership basis. Whenever we had any query or there were changes in law or accounting standards, they would guide our team and set up the process, which would then be followed meticulously. I found this system very effective. In view of low attrition in SsangYong, many in my team had worked for over 25 years. They had really witnessed tough times and had seen the company go bankrupt more than once.

Women in Corporate

In SsangYong, I realized that there were no women at the executive/director position; at best, they were GMs. Till 2020, there was no compulsion to have women directors on the board of listed companies as in India. This was unlike Mahindra & Mahindra in India, where there were quite a few women in senior leadership roles. I ended up with mixed feelings about the place of women in Korea. At the work place, whenever my secretary was absent, a woman employee even at a DGM level was expected to serve tea to guests, even in the presence of junior male employees. I found it very disturbing and stopped this practice in my department. I would rather request guests to help themselves from the vending machine. However, I did meet women in leadership roles in foreign banks and as CFOs in MNCs, who were also keen golfers.

Sudha met many Korean women who were well-educated and had promising careers, which they gave up to take care of their children. Lack of child-care facilities and the culture of working long hours were the main reasons for women quitting their jobs. They said it was very difficult to get back to work after their children grew up, and they faced discrimination of some sort or the other during their working days. 'It is not easy to be a woman in Korea, Sudha-ssi,' they would lament.

At home, women seemed to manage the finances. Most of my colleagues, including senior executives, would make it a point to transfer their entire salary to their wives' account as soon as it was credited and would then receive an allowance for personal expenses. Sudha learnt this from her friends and expected me to transfer my salary to her account. But I jokingly told her that there could be tax issues, and continued my earlier practice of managing family finances along with the company's. When my Korean colleagues came to know about it, they would say, 'You are so lucky that you don't have to ask your wife for an allowance!'

Strong Labour Union Culture

It was only in the 1980s, when the country transitioned to a more democratic political system, that labour activism arose in Korea. It was hitherto restricted and controlled by the authoritarian government. Initially, labour unions were very aggressive, and I was told that violence was common. SsangYong also had experienced a violent strike before Mahindra & Mahindra acquired the company. On the one hand, there were the powerful chaebols, and on the other, there were aggressive labour unions. The government had to intervene on many occasions and walk a tightrope to ensure employee rights were protected while also ensuring that business and the economy were not impacted.

The automobile industry was known to have a strong labour union culture, led by the labour unions of market leaders like Hyundai and Kia. Before going to Korea, a Mahindra & Mahindra colleague who had worked earlier in SsangYong had cautioned me that the labour union could be quite belligerent. There was one incident before I went to Korea when some labour union members had gone to the CFO's office demanding something and started banging the table to intimidate him. Fortunately, I did not experience anything of that sort, though our Korean HR director had to face the music at times.

When I had joined Mahindra & Mahindra in the early 1980s, we had strong labour unions and the evil of working overtime, which led to inefficiencies. Workers used to earn much more than managers. But overtime working was almost eliminated by the late 1990s in Mahindra & Mahindra, leading to remarkable increase in productivity and boost in the morale of officers and managers.

When I came to SsangYong, I was surprised to learn that overtime was very much prevalent in the automobile industry of a developed country like Korea, which impacted its efficiency and morale.

What I found disturbing with our labour union was their reluctance to be flexible to address market needs. When one assembly line was working in top gear with maximum overtime and was still not able to fulfil the demand for its products, another line would remain idle for lack of demand. At times, the labour union leaders would not agree to transfer workmen from one line to another to address the demand. In a competitive environment, this inflexibility was unpardonable. With rising costs and no increase in revenue, no wonder, then, that SsangYong's employee cost as percentage of revenue was way above Mahindra & Mahindra's and of other global automobile companies.

While the R&D, quality and production systems were quite advanced in Korea, the labour unions posed a challenge to progress and growth. There were 40 members of the labour union who did not have to work but were assigned tasks to monitor different areas. So, we had some tracking customer service, R&D work, purchase activities and accounts, and many others monitoring production-related issues and employee grievances. Mind you, these union members were well informed, be it about events within the company or market place or emerging global trends.

Every year, management executives from various departments had to make a presentation to labour union members about new product strategy, new markets, new technology and investments, and answer difficult questions posed by union members. In a lighter vein, I used to say that these meetings were tougher than any board meeting. Once, our exports head was grilled on his return from a foreign country and asked how many vehicles' sales orders he got for the travel expense incurred. On other occasions, the R&D and manufacturing heads were taken to task for quality issues. I realized that the labour union was like a strong opposition party, keeping the management on its toes, but at the same time, stifling growth.

Unlike in India, where we had wage negotiations once in four years, in South Korea, we had wage negotiations every year and collective bargaining to negotiate employee benefits every alternate year. This was an industry-wide practice and there was not much one could do about it. Every year, from May to July, precious management time was spent on these meetings with the labour union where, apart from the HR and manufacturing heads, even the CEO, CFO, and sales, R&D and purchase heads had to be present.

When I asked our CEO why we had to attend all these meetings, he simply said that it was the normal practice; even the CEO of Hyundai attended wage negotiation meetings. My Indian friend, who was a CEO in another company, was able to change this practice. Their company's labour union president told him that he should attend all labour meetings and respect Korean culture. But my friend made it clear to him that the company was not a Korean one and was owned by a foreign company, so it should adopt global best practices. Saying this, he refused to attend wage negotiation meetings.

The end result used to be a 2–4 per cent increase in wages, like we have dearness allowance increase in India, and some negotiations over the annual bonus. I had to attend these meetings with my interpreter, and perhaps address a query or two in the day-long meeting. Once, the labour union leader looked at me and spoke for about a minute. I was waiting for my interpreter to translate as usual, but there was silence. She was sitting next to me. I whispered to her asking about what the leader had said. She said she could not explain since he was talking badly about me and Mahindra & Mahindra. For once, I was glad I did not understand Korean and could not respond. Ignorance was bliss indeed.

Besides wage-negotiation meetings, there were other long meetings to discuss and resolve issues like reinstatement of dismissed workmen, profit-sharing formula, and how to compensate and manage the 52-hour week introduced by the Korean government. Reinstatement of about 150 workmen who were dismissed before Mahindra & Mahindra's acquisition, a decision that was approved by the courts was a hot issue for years, with lot of protests outside the gate and covered by the media.

I remember one incident that occurred when Mr Anand Mahindra had come to Seoul for a product launch. One of the dismissed workmen had climbed a chimney in the factory and was up there for more than a month in the harsh winter (-10 degrees Celsius) to attract attention and seek a solution. Fortunately, he came down after he was assured that the local management will speak to him and look into his grievances sympathetically. I have not seen such tenacity anywhere else. A few years later, all the dismissed workmen were reinstated as a goodwill gesture, despite the fact that they had lost their case in the Supreme Court.

In the seven years of wage-negotiation meetings that I was part of, I saw different styles of leadership in the three labour union presidents. The first one was full of drama and high-pitched theatrics; the second was cool like a cucumber but very firm; and the third seemed to be reasonable and well-mannered and understood the company's difficulties. All these leaders understood that the company was not doing well, but they were always under pressure to show to the workmen that they had got something from the management for the benefit of the employees and kept comparing us with Korean automobile giants Hyundai and Kia.

Labour laws in Korea tend to be pro-workers, and court rulings are also along similar lines in many cases. One example comes to mind. A senior Korean executive in my Indian friend's company was asked to leave for non-performance in 2015. In our company, many executives, whose contracts were only for a year, lost their jobs for various reasons including non-performance. But in this case, the said executive challenged the company and took it to court. The court ruled that the executive could not be dismissed and should be given a chance to improve.

Years rolled by, and the executive was given a chance to improve and continued to get his salary, of course, without increments and bonus. My friend said that the sheer presence of this executive in the office, doing nothing, spoiled the office atmosphere. But they were helpless. It was even suggested that he need not come to office and he would continue to get his salary. But that would have meant people finding out he is not going to office, which does not go down well in Korean culture. When the executive was offered a transfer with a different role, he demanded promotion. And when refused, he stayed put.

To make matters worse, a few years ago, when my friend was in India, a court summons was sent to his residence. As he was travelling, it could not be attended to on time. When he returned, he was stopped at the airport entry, as there was a red flag against his name on the system. He had to spend the next couple of hours at the airport waiting for his company lawyer to sort out the issue.

The court case continues till today and the executive continues to go to office, has his meals there and gets his salary. Some people are indeed thick-skinned.

After we returned to India, I heard a new law was passed called Serious Accidents Prevention Act (SAPA), whereby any serious accident in the company resulting in death was to be treated as a criminal offence and that the CEO of the company could be put in prison. Despite various representations from companies and associations, I understand that the law remains, hanging as a Damocles Sword over the head of every CEO.

After Office Hours

What is life like after office hours in Korea? Most Koreans continue to work after dinner, at least they did in our office. I had once read that in Japan, one of the reasons most office-going people work till late is because their houses are small. But that may not be the case in Korea. Many times, there dare deadlines to be met, but in many cases it is also peer pressure. It depends on the seniors. If they are in office, their juniors will not leave the office before them. Especially if the seniors belong to the older generation, which was the case in our company, they will expect others to work late.

But wait, there is some relief. There is a budget for team leaders and seniors to take their teams out to dinner, to help them bond, once or twice a month. At first, I was surprised to hear about this budget for team dinners because it was not prevalent in Mahindra & Mahindra, India. But then I could see its value in Korea. In office, seniors or bosses and their team members are all very busy and formal, but they open up in these team dinners over soju, beer and food. Juniors are very respectful in office, but I have heard of incidents where some vent their feelings during these team dinners. Of course, there is banter and joking too, but sometimes it can turn serious if a frustrated employee confronts his boss. Fortunately, I always had fun during team dinners and got to know my team members better.

I also learnt Korean drinking etiquettes from my colleagues during the team dinners. When someone is pouring the drink for you, you hold the glass respectfully with both hands. When you pour a drink for others, your one hand rests on the elbow of the serving hand or you hold the bottle with both hands. I always found this action graceful. You are not supposed to fill your own glass but let someone else, usually the person sitting next to you, fill it; or a senior or elder pours the drink for you. Many times, I would forget this after the first drink and, out of habit, would take a bottle to pour into my glass. Then, someone next to me would apologize, take the bottle from me and pour my drink. If a junior colleague is drinking with their senior, out of respect, they will usually look away and not face the senior while sipping their drink.

One thing that puzzled my CEO and other Koreans was the prevalence of vegetarianism among Indians. While Koreans generally eat all types of meat, when it came to us seven Indians from Mahindra & Mahindra in Korea, we were all different. One was a vegan, another vegetarian-not-even-eggs, one ate eggs, another ate fish, or ate fish and chicken but no pork or beef like me, and one ate all types of meat like the Koreans. In this scenario, the Koreans were perplexed – they could digest their meat but not Indian diversity.

After dinner, Koreans like to go for a 'second round'. At first, I did not understand what it meant but after more than one year, I came to know that it meant going to 'noraebang' (karaoke bar) to sing.

There are many noraebangs in Korea; every locality will have more than one near subway stations. One goes in a group and hires a room equipped with karaoke music and a screen for a specified time. One can order some drinks and snacks, and sing to one's heart's content. I found most of my team members to be excellent singers who could belt out Korean songs and sometimes English ones too. Noraebangs are popular across ages. Families and friends visit noraebangs to spend quality time, and thus many Koreans learn to sing well at an early age. There are different types of noraebangs: some that families visit, some where groups of friends sing, and in some, girls join the group to sing and dance at an extra cost.

At formal company dinners, what I liked the most was the practice of raising a toast. We were about 10 employees in the leadership team, along with the CEO. Almost all of us got to speak while raising a toast. Of course, mine would be short and in English, but all the others spoke in Korean and said something interesting and funny, followed by loud cheers and applause. I realized that this was a nice way to get everyone to speak; otherwise, many times in a large group, all do not get a chance to speak. The Korean word for cheers is 'geonbae'. I used to introduce myself as 'Tumbe, just like geonbae'. That made it easy for Koreans to remember my name.

Once, during our senior leadership team dinner, our CEO asked me, 'What do you say for cheers in any Indian language?' I said, 'There is no other word, we say cheers.' He was not ready to accept my answer, and insisted that there must be an Indian word. I said, 'I cannot think of any other word. It is cheers only.' Then he suggested that there must be a word for ultimate satisfaction or bliss. At that moment, Lord Buddha came to my mind but I forgot the word 'nirvana' and instead said that a word for such an experience is 'moksha'. After that, for the next three or four rounds, everyone said moksha instead of cheers! I was embarrassed, but I was the only Indian in the group, so it did not matter much. After a few months, our Indian boss came to Seoul and, during a formal dinner, our CEO and others started saying 'moksha' for cheers. He was completely baffled. I had to explain the background, and we had a good laugh.

The older generation of Koreans seem to drink much more than the younger one. I could be wrong. Perhaps, the younger generation is shy, or drinks less out of respect. Maybe they'd be different with their friends. But I did come across young people who did not drink alcohol at all. I guess the older generation has worked hard all their lives and work and peer pressures make them drink more. In India and elsewhere too, people have different types of drinks based on their budgets and social standing. What I found remarkable was that, in Korea, while people may have different drinks to suit their wallets, soju is a universal drink had by all. Be it the CEO of a company or the junior most employee, all will have soju. They might have it by itself, or mixed with beer or whisky.

It is an accepted practice that after a party, one or two will need to be helped into a taxi and dropped home. But what surprised me was that the next day, everyone is in office on time. I later came to know that they have a special soup in the morning to overcome a hangover.

Playing Golf

My colleagues were coaxing me to start playing golf so that I could socialize with my bankers, as was the practice. But I was hesitant and did not know where and how to start. I asked a colleague from my department to help me find a place to practise in an indoor facility with golf simulators. He searched online and gave me an address that turned out to be in my apartment complex itself. I was not aware of it, since the signboards were in Korean. I practised for a month, with the help of a coach who knew only Korean. The facility was not designed for a left-hander like me and, with the language issue, my progress was slow. In fact, Sudha suggested that I should play with my right-hand, since they did not have the facility and kit for left handers. I tried, but once a left-hander, always a left-hander.

One day, after dinner, my office colleagues Lee Soo-won and G.W. Park took me to a proper indoor golf simulator facility to play a game, and with their help I enjoyed golf for the first time. Lee Soo-won, a left-hander like me, took special interest in teaching me the basics and was kind enough to gift me a golf club to motivate me to practise. I frequented these indoor facilities for a few more months, before stepping onto a golf course. My colleagues helped me get the golf clubs for left-handers, balls, shoes and gloves, and explained the etiquettes of the golf course.

Thereafter, I must have played at a golf course about 15 times with colleagues and bankers, and enjoyed the ambience and surroundings in different locations around Seoul. I realized that I have to unlearn my cricket bat swing while playing golf. However much I tried, I would slice my drives and the ball would curl away instead of going straight. So, I started aiming my drives at 60 degrees (like mid-on position in cricket) and the ball would go straight. The other players were amused at this adaptation. Due to the rising popularity of golf, there are many golf courses in Korea. They are well maintained but on the expensive side as compared to the US.

Playing golf takes almost the whole day: one-hour's drive each way to some scenic golf course, four–five hours' play, followed by beer and lunch or dinner. I enjoyed playing, and it helped me bond with colleagues and bankers. I also enjoyed playing in the indoor golf simulators that take less time and are common in many localities across Seoul. After returning to India, I am yet to find an indoor golfing facility in Mumbai and golf courses are few and far, as a result of which I have not played golf since then.

Indian Expat Colleagues and Friends

One saving grace of living in a new country like Korea was that we were seven expats from Mahindra & Mahindra, India, living close by. We were great support to one another and to the families. We were seven Indians among 5,000 Korean employees at SsangYong at any given time. Over 10 years, there were about 17 expats, as some returned after a stint of three or four years and were replaced. Somesh, Dilip, Prahlada, Joydeep, Virendra, Punit, Ramdas and Sundar had been living in Korea since 2011, and helped me settle in quickly in the country.

While I had a driver and travelled by myself to work, others went together in a company vehicle. I missed their interesting discussions on a variety of topics during their hour-long ride to the factory. Of course, they shared the highlights of their discussions for my benefit during lunch in the factory canteen, which would get vegetarian food from an Indian restaurant. Since all of us were in different functions, we got a perspective of what was happening across the company and learnt a lot. Once or twice a week, I would go to our office at Gangnam, where our finance, sales and exports departments were located. My colleague

Sanjeev, who worked in the exports department, would join me and we would have interesting conversations on a wide range of topics, including our exports business, while travelling or having lunch.

Many times, one of our colleagues' wives would go to India. For example, Sudha would go to India during winter for three months. On such occasions, we would have a 'boys' party' on weekends at the temporary bachelor's place with our karaoke set-up. We had some good singers like Satish, Chandrakant, Pavan, Ashutosh, Sameer and Rahul, which made the evenings lively. On some weekends, we played indoor games like bowling, baseball or golf on a simulator.

Our colleagues Satish and Shankar drove 20 km on weekends to play badminton, whereas Sundar and Chandrakant drove over 50 km to play cricket. There was an annual cricket tournament, where we had teams with players from India, Pakistan, Bangladesh, England and Australia vying for the top honour.

There were about 10,000 Indians in Korea at the time, spread throughout the country. Some worked in Korean companies like Samsung, LG, Hyundai and Cupoung (the Amazon of Korea), some were in the ship-building industry, and many were professors or academics doing research in Korean universities. There were a few representing big Indian companies like Mahindra & Mahindra, Tata, Aditya Birla Group's Novelis, State Bank of India and a few MNCs. There was a merchant community, mostly trading in textiles, who had been living in Korea for more than 30 years. They formed the Indian Merchants Association and organized events to celebrate Indian festivals like Navratri.

A few enterprising Indians had also started their own businesses in Korea.

Shyam Paliwal, a close friend, came to Korea when he was working on one of the largest liquefied natural gas carriers in the world. He then met a Korean girl whom he married, and decided to stay on in Korea. Today, he is a trainer in that field and a speaker at conferences. He saw a growing demand for Indian cuisine in Korea and started his first restaurant. He faced many challenges, and was quick to adapt and cater to Korean tastes. Today, he has a chain of 12 restaurants named Bombay Brau in different parts of the country. In 2018, Shyam realized that there was a market for craft beer in Korea, and acquired a brewery in Busan. He is now selling craft beer named Praha993. Interestingly, 993 AD is the year when the first brewery was started in Praha (Prague) in the Czech Republic. Shyam is settled in Busan, where he pursues his other passion – sailing. He does so on his own yacht with his family and friends. We have many pleasant memories together in Seoul as well as in Busan.

Another friend became a famous personality on a TV show, anchored the Indian Chamber of Commerce in Korea's (ICCK's) annual Diwali Ball event more than once and now owns a restaurant to capitalize on his brand value. Our friend, Pankaj Agarwal, an IIT and Harvard Business School alumnus, started an IIT Alumni Association in Korea. Additionally, after working with Samsung Electronics, he started his own venture – an education technology company called Tag Hive.

We celebrated Indian festivals like Ganapati, Dusshera, Diwali and Holi with some of the Indian community members in Korea. There was an association called Indians in Korea full of young, enthusiastic Indians who took the initiative to organize various events. For Holi, the organizers had to take prior permission to celebrate the festival of colours by the Han River in the open. The temperature was below 10 degrees Celsius. The permission given was for a fixed time on payment of a deposit, and one was supposed to keep the music within prescribed decibel levels and had to clean up the place before departing. It was nice to see some Koreans attending this festival and enjoying with the Indian community.

Ganapati and Diwali were celebrated with great pomp, showcasing the talents of the Indian community, including the children, be it in music, in dance or in the culinary filed. These events had the blessings of the Indian Embassy in Korea, and the Ambassador or their deputy would grace the occasion. The Indian Embassy organized a month-long cultural festival called 'Sarang', bringing famous singers, musicians and chefs from India. This was appreciated by the Koreans and the Indian diaspora. We all looked forward to this annual event that showcased a wide range of music and dance performances by maestros, and had a variety of delicious Indian-cuisine recipes dished out by chefs from India.

The Indian Chamber of Commerce in Korea

The ICCK was established in 2010 at the initiative of the Indian Embassy in Korea to promote India–Korea trade. By virtue of SsangYong being a charter member of the ICCK,

I was nominated to its board in 2013. It was a fantastic learning experience to interact with other business heads at the board meetings. Our then chairman, Shashi Maudgal, started an initiative of Saturday meetings, where different individuals made presentations about their businesses in Korea. This was a great way to understand how business was conducted in the country from different company perspectives. In 2015, Prime Minister (PM) Narendra Modi visited Korea, which was an exciting moment for all of us.

In July 2017, I was appointed as the chairman of the ICCK, a position I held till December 2019. This was a challenging and exciting task for me in many ways. On the one hand, the ICCK's focus was to increase membership and revenue to become self-sustaining, and on the other, it wanted to promote and enhance India–Korea trade and investment.

The ICCK, with the help of the Indian Embassy, organized road-shows for various Indian state governments, where they could showcase what they had to offer to attract Korean investment. These events were typically two to three hours of presentations, followed by one-on-one business meetings with prospective clients. I was privileged to meet many chief ministers and industry ministers from various states, and got an insight into the progress they were making, which was indeed very impressive. For example, as I was living in Korea, I was not fully aware of the rapid progress being made in infrastructure, the speed at which roads were getting constructed and that some states had become power surplus and were even supporting other states. If I got their presentations in advance, I insisted on making one correction – from lakh and crore to million and billion.

Prime Minister Modi visited Korea again in February 2019, and this time I had the privilege of getting a picture of the ICCK team with him. There was a business meet in the afternoon where the PM gave a very inspiring speech for half an hour. In the evening, PM Modi was to address the Indian diaspora. About 15 groups of 15–20 people each were lined up in the hall for a photograph with the PM, including our ICCK team. I thought to myself, even if he takes only five minutes with each group, it will take more than an hour before he addresses the audience.

At the appointed time, in strode PM Modi with the Ambassador, stood for the photograph with our team and asked a question as we were getting clicked. In 30 seconds, he was done and had moved to the next group. He could cover all the groups within ten minutes. During his talk to the Indian diaspora, he exhorted each Indian to convince at least five Korean friends to visit India, which could help boost tourism in India. I found that PM Modi left his mark not only on the Indian diaspora but also on the Koreans who had attended. It felt nice when many Koreans told me later how fortunate we were to have a strong PM.

The ICCK also arranged to take some Korean businesses to India once a year to meet prospective clients in places like Delhi, Chennai and Mumbai. I realized that our Secretary General had been to India many times when he told me that he had been to Agra to see the Taj Mahal nine times!

There were other events the ICCK arranged, like breakfast meetings called Speaker's Forum, where we invited interesting speakers; networking events with the Ambassador; and the flagship event Diwali Ball, a much-awaited marquee event on Seoul's social calendar. This event was attended by 400 people that included diplomats, CEOs, bankers, lawyers, businessmen and artists. We showcased India and the festival of lights with a delightful dance performance by artists flown in from India and Indian chefs dishing out delicious Indian delicacies.

In 2017, the Diwali Ball was held on 11 November, a day that is celebrated in Korea as Pepero Day. Pepero is a brand of chocolate-dipped sticks that are exchanged by the young on this day, as 11/11 can be depicted by four sticks like Pepero. This celebration is similar to Valentine's Day, and marketers have capitalized on its popularity. For the Diwali Ball, we added Pepero in the guests' goodie bags, much to their delight.

It was such an exhilarating feeling when the guests exclaimed that our Diwali Ball was far superior to the American or French Chamber Annual Ball. Our team worked untiringly – getting sponsorships and selling tables, getting the dance troupe of 20 from India, arranging the logistics, planning the flow of the event, selecting and testing the menu, the table arrangements (where we gave names of Indian states or cities to each table to familiarize Koreans with India) and, of course, organizing a DJ to play Hindi and English music, among other things. I always wondered how a small team of three in the ICCK could pull off such a grand event!

Work–Life Imbalance?

While speaking to Korean businessmen, I felt that they still carried the baggage of the failure of POSCO to set up the mega project in Odisha, and were hesitant to invest in India. I used to tell them that POSCO has moved on with a smaller project in India. With China slowing down, they should focus on investing in India. The biggest advantage, I told them, is that India has a stable democratic government, a young, dynamic population, and is expanding rapidly in areas of infrastructure and technology. When they had questions about investment in India, I advised them that while there could be a central policy at the union government-level in Delhi, they should closely study the state in which they were interested, since India is a diverse country and each state is like a country with its own language, food, customs and culture.

While India–Korea trade did increase from USD 16 billion in 2015 to USD 20 billion in 2019, I was surprised to note that for Koreans, India ranked below Vietnam and Indonesia when it came to trade and investment. A study in 2018 revealed that there were about 500 Korean businesses registered in India, most of them wholly owned subsidiaries, as compared to the 5,000 Korean businesses in Vietnam. It will be worthwhile to see what Vietnam is doing right to attract investment. One thing I know is that approvals happen faster in Vietnam, and Koreans like speed and action – palli palli.

My work experience in Korea was good, maybe because I was on the same side as the Koreans. When I spoke to some friends in India who had business dealings with Koreans, their experience was not so great. While language was one issue, they also found Koreans to be too demanding, workaholics and only interested in achieving their objective without a care for building or maintaining good relations. In Korea, they value relationships a lot, but perhaps only among fellow Koreans. Besides, I realized my friends were dealing with employees of big Korean companies who tend to have an attitude of superiority.

Having an interpreter in office and an English-speaking driver outside made my life in Korea easy and enjoyable. But what about my wife? How did she manage without a car or a driver and, more importantly, without a work visa after being busy 24x7 in India? Did she enjoy as much in Korea? Sudha will explain.

5
Life Without a Work Visa

When we visited Korea in March 2013 for a 'look and see', I really liked the country and wished to be able to live there for a few years. The people seemed friendly and I thought to myself that, if I learnt their language I will be able to make new friends and understand their culture better.

Vasudev's factory was nearly 50 km from our house, and he would be out and busy for 12 hours of the day. I did not have a work visa, did not know the language and did not know where and how to begin. Our 30-storey apartment had no other foreigners, only Koreans. Language was an issue. Smile was the universal language. In the elevator, in the lobby, people would look at me curiously and ask, 'Indo?' I would just smile and bow occasionally. I could sense that they wanted to converse with me, so I would ask, 'English?' They would say no with a gesture of crossed hands, and I would move on. I made up my mind to learn Korean to be able to converse with them.

Vasudev's company had organized basic Korean-language learning at Gangnam. The metro station was a five-minute walk from our place. I started taking the metro to Gangnam station to attend Korean-language classes. Our Korean teacher did not know English, but she was fluent in Chinese, which did not help me. We were forced to speak only in Korean, which, in a way, was good for the cause of learning the language.

I started exploring nearby convenience stores, GS and E Mart. Everything was written in Korean. Sometimes, I would be lucky to meet someone who knew some English. Vasudev does not like to go shopping, and would get irritated whenever I stepped into a store just to enquire. Later, he understood the real reason behind my enquiries, which was to speak Korean with the store's staff and read labels. They were, in a way, part of me learning the language.

I made my first friends in Korea through the class: Keiko from Japan, Lisa Lee from Hong Kong and Daniel from Columbia. We started hanging out in coffee shops after class where we practised our Korean without any inhibition, since we were all in the same boat. We also got to know each other better; I came to know more about their countries, and they had many questions to ask about India.

Our class was only for a month and we parted ways, as they left for their respective countries. Nevertheless, we continued to stay in touch through social media. Lisa Lee had married a Korean and, hence, wanted to learn the language to converse with her in-laws. After a few months, they moved to England. In 2023, when we were in London, they drove all the way from Birmingham with their toddler and pet dog just to meet us over a cup of coffee. When I asked Lisa why she went through the trouble of travelling and staying in a hotel, she remarked, 'What! I would not have missed this chance to meet you after 10 years.' I was deeply touched by this. Vasudev asked me, 'How long did you know her in Korea?' I said, 'Maybe two months.'

Keiko left for Japan, but before that, she gave me two inputs that were to change my life in Korea and for which I am ever grateful to her. Since our Korean-language class got over after a month, she told me that some of her Japanese friends went to the Yeoksam Global Village Center to learn Korean, and that it was free of cost. The second suggestion was that I should become a member of the Seoul International Women's Association (SIWA) to connect with expats and other Koreans.

Global Center

As suggested by Keiko, one day, I went to visit Yeoksam Global Village Center near Gangnam to find out whether I could join their class. To my delight, the next batch at the Center was about to start the following week; I enrolled myself immediately. I came to know that there were many such centres in different parts of Seoul, which serve as community centres for Koreans, especially the elderly, and foreign nationals. These centres have libraries, mostly with Korean books, gymnasiums with state-of-the-art equipment and basic medical facilities. They also organize many activities. For foreigners, they have Korean classes, driving license training facilities and legal or taxation related advice. All this is free or for a very nominal charge.

I made the most of what the Center had to offer for the next six years. I started going for Korean-language classes twice a week using the metro, a 20-minute ride from my place to Gangnam.

I had seen the Hindi movie *English Vinglish* right before coming to Seoul, and could relate to the movie and the lead actress Sridevi while going to the class. Coming back from the class, I would say to Vasudev, 'I am back from my "Korean-Worean" class.'

These classes are free for all levels, from the very first level till TOPIK, the Korean-language proficiency test. The minimum requirements were 70 per cent attendance and 70 per cent passing marks. Over the years, I studied up to the final level and also learnt business Korean.

The Korean language is made up of 24 letters, known as 'Hangul', with 10 vowels and 14 consonants. In ancient times, Koreans used the Chinese script. As it was very difficult, only the intelligent, elite, upper-class people (known as 'Yangban') working in the king's court received higher education. In 1443, King Se-jong created the present-day Hangul system, which was a simplified version, and offered it to the public on 10 October 1443. Due to its simplicity, the level of literacy increased exponentially. Today, 10 October is a national holiday called 'Hangul Day', when essay and elocution competitions are conducted.

I remember our teacher telling us on the first day that Korean is so simple that if you do not get the letters right in the first week, then you must be really very slow or something must be wrong with you. I guess this was her way of motivating us or putting pressure on us. Indeed, the letters were simple, and I started remembering them within a week.

That was just the beginning. The fun started when we began constructing sentences, with the awkward pronunciations by students from different countries. Soon, I realized that I should not think in English but in an Indian language to get the sentence right. For example, 'What is your name?' is written as 'Your name what is?' in Korean, Hindi and Marathi. We all laughed in the class when our teacher said 'uri nampyeon' to mean 'my husband' because we had just learnt that 'uri nara' means 'our country', so when we were thinking in English we translated as '*our* husband'. Later, I realized that it is just like we say in Hindi, 'hamare pati'.

There are some words in Korean that people from English-speaking or Western countries cannot pronounce. The word for water is 'mool' but the pronunciation does not have the common 'l' and instead comes with a twist of the tongue. I could pronounce it perfectly because Indian languages like Marathi, based on Sanskrit, have a similar alphabet. Although I speak Marathi at home, I found the tone of the Korean language similar to Kannada. So, I started using my Kannada tone while speaking Korean, and later my Korean friends started saying, 'Oh! She speaks like one of us.'

Our class had people from different countries and age groups. Some were working-professionals, some were students and some were wives of expats. I had one classmate who was born Korean but had been adopted by US citizens. She had come to Seoul to find her roots and to learn the native language. Nobody asked about educational qualification – everyone was in the class to learn Korean from the first level.

Our Korean teacher was very patient and understanding. She knew only Korean. Many classmates were from non-non-English-speaking countries like Russia, China, Japan and France. We were forced to converse only in Korean in the class. But we were just beginners. We used our hands, frantic gestures and desperate facial expressions to express the words we wanted to communicate. It was as if we were all playing a game of dumb charades. Nobody else understood us but our teacher, somehow, always managed to get the gist and encouraged us. The scene in the class was quite like the English TV series *Mind Your Language* or its Hindi avatar *Zaban Sambhal Ke*! We all had to control our laughter, as our teacher would be serious and correct us patiently. This gave us confidence and we were not shy to speak even if we made mistakes.

The lessons comprised describing our daily activities, for which we had to make our own sentences. It was quite a revelation to know how people from different countries and cultures think about and express their daily activities. For example, when I was explaining making breakfast for my husband and cooking before coming for the class, many, including my Korean teacher, were surprised that I cooked at home regularly. At first, I did not understand why, but later I came to know that a majority of them seldom cooked but ate at their workplace or in restaurants.

One common theme I observed was the national pride exhibited by all. We were supposed to talk about our country's culture, festivals and food. I explained Diwali to my classmates in Korean, of course more with gestures and expressions than words, and distributed Indian sweets and snacks. More than learning the language, during the initial period, I learnt more about the customs and cultures of different countries of Europe, South America and Asia (especially China and Japan) thanks to the diversity in the classroom. Most of my classmates talked about the four seasons in their countries and were surprised when I told them we had only three seasons in India – summer, monsoon and winter.

After the class, we would go for coffee. Even our teacher would sometimes join us, and continued to guide us and solved our queries. Once, our teacher mentioned the importance of knowing a language like English, which has global appeal, and how Koreans learnt Mandarin as China's clout increased on the international scene. Now, she wanted to learn an Indian language, Hindi, as India is likely to take global centre stage in the future. I was overwhelmed to hear this glowing comment about India in front of so many foreigners in the class. My classmates became more curious about India thereafter and wanted to know more about it.

While most of them were from non-English-speaking countries and were naturally proficient in their country's language, they were puzzled to see me talk to my Indian friend in English and not an Indian language. I had to explain to them that, in India, we have many languages across different states or provinces and even though we have Hindi as a common language, some people from South India do not speak it. Hence, many times, English is the only common language for Indians.

At the Center, I also made the most of the other activities like painting, handicraft, calligraphy, cooking and excursions. 'Minhwa' is an integral part of Korean culture. It literally means 'painting of the people' or 'popular painting'. We used to admire wonderful nature paintings on the walls and ceilings of Buddhist temples. I started going to the Yeoksam Global Village Center to learn Minhwa painting. What makes this art more unique is that the paints are made from natural elements like stones or powdered seashells. Birds and flowers like lotus are the most common designs, and we learnt to paint on ceramic pots, plates and hanji, a special type of traditional Korean paper. Our teachers were very patient and encouraged me to use brushes with a steady hand and calm mind. As someone who was never fond of drawing or painting in school or thereafter, I started enjoying it and surprised myself and Vasudev with some nice paintings that adorn our walls till today. The icing on the cake was when a close Indian friend specifically asked for a painting for his home in India.

I also learnt the craft of making objects using hanji like pen stands, lamp shades and boxes, since the paper is sturdy and gives the effect of natural wood. This paper is so strong that in traditional Korean hanoks, the walls, doors and windows are made of hanji. A renowned handicraft artist gifted me a lovely box made of hanji. I was told that this box was traditionally used to store rice by the less privileged, while the rich stored money in it. In my house in India, it is full of precious Korean memories.

I also got a chance to learn about 'jagae' or mother-of-pearl art, which are inlaid on lacquered objects like plates, pots, traditional cupboards, tables and jewellery boxes. These items look attractive and are popular souvenirs for tourists, especially the jewellery boxes that come in different sizes and are quite expensive.

The Seoul Global Cultural Center at downtown Myeongdong also had Korean cooking classes. I am not a very enthusiastic cook, but this was my chance to learn something new. I had developed a taste for Korean food. In the first year, I was a vegetarian and restricted myself to kimchi, bibimbap, kimbap and japchae, which were supposed to be vegetarian items.

When I joined the cooking class, the first dish they taught us to make was the famous kimchi. I was very excited. Kimchi is a side dish comprising salted and fermented cabbage, topped with a traditional Korean sauce. I was surprised when the teacher explained that the sauce that is added to the cabbage is fish sauce! I was happily eating Kimchi till then, assuming it was vegetarian because my Korean friends consider fish to be vegetarian. Then I came to know that most bakery products like biscuits, breads and cakes contain egg. When we went to an Indian restaurant, even the naan had egg. After kimchi, we learnt to make kimbap, which is rice with vegetables wrapped in seaweed. After realizing that I had been eating eggs and fish unknowingly, I decided to eat non-vegetarian food gradually, to the delight of my Korean friends.

The Yeoksam Global Village Center arranged many excursions free of cost to nearby places, explaining their significance. I would wear a saree or salwar-kameez, which attracted attention. Thanks to my clothes, people's curiosity grew and I got to field a lot of questions about India.

Once, when my son's family had come to visit us, they joined me for an excursion to a strawberry garden, where we got to experience everything from picking strawberries to actually making our own jam. My five-year-old grandson enjoyed the trip a lot.

Temple stay is very popular in Korea. With the Yeoksam Global Village Center group, I got the opportunity to visit a Buddhist temple and stay overnight to experience their food and meditation. The thatched-roof design, the calm face of the Buddha, the mountain backdrop, the silence, the cleanliness – all of it was very comforting.

The experience I cherish the most was of our stay with a Korean family in a hanok in a far-off village. That day was my mother's birthday, and I got to meet an old couple and a grandmother who, coincidentally, turned out to be my mother's age. We sat on the floor and, over traditional food, discussed the journeys of their lives. As is common in most countries, including India, this couple's children were working in bigger cities and visited them only during festivals. I was impressed with the cleanliness in the village and the hospitality shown by our hosts. While leaving, they urged me to bring my mother next time. I was truly touched.

Once, the Yeoksam Global Village Center organized a trip to a place to visit 'comfort women'. We were explained the history of how young Korean girls were taken by the ruling Japanese to China and Japan during War time under the pretext of giving them jobs as nurses but, in effect, using them as 'comfort women'. The Korean government had pressurized the Japanese government for a formal apology on the 'comfort women' issue, which the Japanese government had initially refused. This led to a lot of public anger in Korea against Japan for some time, and Koreans boycotted Japanese goods and shops at the height of the issue.

Very few of the 'comfort women' are alive today, and we were taken to visit two old ladies in their nineties, who had gone through the ordeal. We were given strict instructions not to ask them any questions related to their past. When I met these ladies, I was too overwhelmed to say anything. I just took one lady's hand and managed to introduce myself in Korean, 'I am Sudha from India.' She gave a weak smile and pointed to the cap I was wearing. I gave the cap to her as a memento, and she happily posed for a photo with me after wearing my cap. This encounter with the old lady is etched in my memory.

I made many international friends at the Yeoksam Global Village Center over the years, and we enjoyed a lot over a cup of coffee after class or during our excursions. Many visited my home to taste home-cooked Indian food and, once, to practise for a dance programme for the annual-day celebrations. Since I was the eldest in the group, some, who were away from their homes, opened their hearts to me for advice.

Before moving back to India, the Yeoksam Global Village Center felicitated me with a certificate, and I owe them a lot for enriching my life in Korea.

Seoul International Women's Association (SIWA)

Seoul International Women's Association is an organization for Koreans returning, after living elsewhere in the world, and for foreign women living in Korea. I had heard about it from some people but, as mentioned before, it was my Japanese friend Keiko who really introduced me to it. It was started in 1962 as a space where women from different countries could connect, share their culture, and use their skill and experience to support one another and those in need. I became a member of SIWA by paying the annual membership fee, and it opened doors for me to network with women from various countries. Most of these women were like me – with no work visa, having come to Korea with their husbands.

The Association arranged networking events, exhibitions and talks by experts, which enabled me to meet and get acquainted with many interesting women. Fundraising events, like the annual bazaar, were organized to support disadvantaged communities. Many Ambassadors' wives arranged luncheon events at their residences to showcase their country's art, music, cuisine and sightseeing places to promote tourism. I got an opportunity to attend some of these meetings. In the process, I became friends with women whom I am in touch through social media even today.

Some of the SIWA members who lived near our place at Bundang, decided to start a smaller group and we called it 'Bundango's'. Jin Hee, Young Mi, Kelly, Barbara, Brigitte, Maria, Krista, Sabine, Anne Marie, Josine, Cecilia, Monica, Helena, Christine and I were Bundango's over a six-year period.

Seoul International Women's Association had a book club that I attended a few times. During one of these meets, an Indian friend in Seoul, Shubha, invited me to join a smaller book club started by Lena. At this book club, I met like-minded ladies who read different kinds of books, which were then discussed when we met. Coming from various countries, Lena, Betty, Neiva, Pauline, Hope, Shubha and Mita gave different perspectives to the discussions on the books we read, all of which I enjoyed thoroughly. Although most of us are back in our respective countries now, we are still in touch and continue to discuss various books that we have read on our WhatsApp group chat.

Thanks to SIWA, I made some life-long friends like Park Yeong-shil, an accomplished author and professor; Helena Kim Ju, president of the World Egg Artists Association; Cecilia Kim, a famous Soprano and professor; Christine Choi, who had returned from New Zealand; Kelly Yoon, who was back from the US; my ever-helpful friend, Yoon Jin-hee; and Monica Park, who introduced me to two associations with whom I then got connected – Anna's House and Korea Dyslexia Association.

Park Yeong-shil was my first Korean friend in Korea, and is now one of my best friends. She is a well-known author. We met at an international book club in Seoul in

October 2013, and after the discussion we went out to have coffee. While introducing herself at the book club, she had said her name was Audrey. I was curious about her English name, and so, once we settled for a cup of coffee, I asked her about it. She explained, 'Korean names are difficult for foreigners to pronounce, so we use English names as nicknames. My Korean name is Yeong-shil, but to make it easy for foreigners I go by Audrey.'

This was new to me because the Koreans I had met so far had told me their Korean names. I told her that I have no problem pronouncing Yeong-shil, and that I will address her as Yeong-shil and not Audrey. That kind of struck a chord in that first meeting. I was her first Indian friend and she wanted to know more about India. It also gave her a chance to practise speaking in English.

As we were finishing our coffees, I asked her, 'Would you like to come to my house?' It was quite far but she readily agreed to come with me, changing two trains. This was her first visit to an Indian's house. As she entered, there was nothing to surprise her, since we had Korean-style furniture, which she was used to. But later, she noticed the Jaipur-style bedsheets and pillow covers as well as our Indian showpieces. She got more curious and started asking questions about India.

After a while, I said I will make her some poha, and showed her what it looks on YouTube. She accompanied me to the kitchen and was surprised to find the kitchen filled with stainless steel items – containers, plates, bowls, cups, spoons in different sizes. Koreans are used to ceramics or glassware, and this was new for Yeong-shil. My mother had gifted me many steel utensils at the time of our marriage, some of which had never been used. We had decided to bring them to Korea. Yeong-shil got very emotional when I showed her the Marathi engraving at the back of the plate, which translates to, 'To Sudha, with best wishes, Nandini Huzurbazar, 4th May 1984.' Yeong-shil said that my mother's memory will come alive whenever I use the utensils, even though my mother had never come to Korea. These words came true when my Korean friends requested that I distribute some of the steel utensils with my mother's name among them as a memento when I was leaving Korea. Yeong-shil enjoyed the poha in a steel plate and a cup of masala tea, which again was new to her, as they were used to having black tea with no milk or sugar.

Over the next few years, we met often at traditional Korean restaurants and had interesting conversations about the books she wrote or was about to write, the books we read, and my Indian life and experiences. She loved the Diwali Ball organized by the ICCK, and wore for the occasion the saree and Indian ornaments I had given her. She has seen India through our conversations and liked it so much that she wants to visit soon. Once, she showed me her new Korean book, *The Manor Club*, where, in the preface, she mentions me and how she saw and understood India through her interactions and friendship with me. I was really touched by her gesture. This motivated me even more to learn Korean, so I could read her books. I learnt a lot about Korea from Yeong-shil, who has authored eight books and is a well-respected professor. We continue to be in touch on KakaoTalk.

Helena Kim Ju is another close friend who introduced me to the world of art and craft in Korea. She is the president of the World Egg Artists Association. Her amazing works of art – with embellishment of precious Swarovski stones on eggs – are exhibited in a hall constructed in an egg shape in Capella Ovi (Cheongran Church), which was built on her initiative, as well as in international exhibitions. Helena, who studied business administration in Korea and helped her husband in his business, had moved to New Zealand for her son's education. As a hobby, she started learning 'egg art', and soon showed her excellence in delicate handiwork. She started displaying her work in exhibitions and earned recognition internationally. She is now a director at the Association of Royal Crafts Culture in Korea, and also works for the Korea Art and Culture Master Association.

As our friendship blossomed, she started sending me pictures of her egg art as well as works of other great artists on social media. I had the privilege of attending various exhibitions with her in Korea. One noteworthy exhibition was in a reputed gallery in Seoul. It warmed our hearts to see even North Korean artists displaying traditional art there. Helena's fine, linear carvings on an ostrich egg were mesmerizing. There is magic in her fingers; even when we go to a restaurant for a cup of coffee or lunch, her hands are unconsciously busy making objects from tissue paper as we talk. Origami must have been her favourite subject.

Once, I went with Helena to meet her friend Lee Jeong-yeol at her studio, Sugar Art Craft. Lee Jeong-yeol is the president of Sugar Atelier, a global sugar-art company. Her cake icing work is simply stunning! On Facebook, her students from all over the world are constantly posting the charming icing art they have learnt from her. It is difficult to believe that the numerous replicas of trees, flowers, cars, people and places, which are kept in the temperature-controlled studio, are made of sugar. I was awestruck. While leaving, I complimented her and said I hoped to continue our 'sweet' friendship.

Traditional artists in Korea get some support from the government to keep their art forms alive. I was touched to receive such artworks with signatures as mementos when we moved back to India. Before our departure, Helena sent a reporter to my place to interview me about my experiences in Korea. This was video recorded by the agency and uploaded on YouTube, and remains a fond memory.[*] I learnt to appreciate art and craft due to my interactions with Helena, and got the opportunity to meet many artistes thanks to her wide network.

These chance encounters with interesting people led me one day to Cecilia Kim, a well-known soprano. She had come for a coffee meeting of the SIWA Bundang group. I liked her candid behaviour and sense of humour, and we clicked from day one. Cecilia Kim is also a music professor in Seoul, having lived in Italy for many years to study Western music and practise opera singing. She returned to Seoul to look after her ageing parents and participates in musical concerts besides teaching music. I

---

[*]YSM TV. 'Sudha Tumbe, 한국생활 스토리 그리고 인사(인도로 되돌아 가며 남긴 인사).' *YouTube*, 24 December 2019, tinyurl.com/bdehfcja.

got many opportunities to attend her concerts, and soon, I developed a taste for Western classical music. It was quite a sight to see Cecilia on stage – confident and elegantly dressed, singing high notes with ease and control, the crowd's applause and shouts of 'bravo' followed by standing ovations after each performance!

Coincidentally, Cecilia's pianists for her concerts were my Russian friend Ellena, who I knew from Yeoksam Global Village Center, and her husband Alexander. I was thrilled to go backstage to greet Cecilia and Ellena after the event. Later, thanks to Cecilia, Vasudev and I got a chance to attend a grand classical music concert hosted by the Italian embassy, which we enjoyed thoroughly.

When we were about to return to India, Cecilia gifted me a unique cloth bag made by her mother. This bag was cut from denim jeans and had a picture of an Indian princess. It was skilfully created using appliques of different pieces of cloth interspersed with jewels. As Cecilia handed me the bag, she said, 'This is for my Indian princess from my mother.' I was overwhelmed. Whenever I use this bag, people invariably ask me about it, which reminds me of my dear friend Cecilia and her late mother. On my return to India, I started listening to Western classical music in addition to my favourite Indian music for which I am ever grateful to Cecilia.

It was Christine Choi who taught me how to shop in the street and metro station markets, and introduced me to a variety of Korean delicacies. After graduating from New Zealand, she quit her job and returned to Korea where she met and married Kevin, a hard-working engineer and supportive husband. The first time I met Christine was when she came for a SIWA coffee meeting with her daughter, Suha, in a pram. I liked her positive, happy attitude and chirpy way of talking, and we became friends instantly! She started calling me 'unni' and later Suha started calling me 'imo'. Kevin and Christine were much younger than us, but we got along very well and visited many restaurants to try out Korean delicacies as recommended by Christine. She introduced me to 'makgeolli', the Korean rice wine usually had with lunch and especially popular among women.

Christine was surprised to know that I had changed my surname after marriage, unlike Korean women. She continued to be Christine Choi after being married to Kevin Kwon, and their daughter was Suha Kwon. I told her most Indian women used to change their surnames after marriage but that this is changing in the younger generation. Women now prefer to retain their maiden surnames or add the husband's surname to their maiden one. In a lighter vein, I told her that I was lucky not to change my first name too, which was also a practice back then. She asked me for my business card, which is the first thing people exchange in Korea, and I said, 'I don't have one, I am a homemaker.' Christine immediately responded, 'So what? Being a homemaker is also an important task. You should have a business card too.' I just smiled and let it pass, but looking back, I do feel that what Christine said made sense.

After sending her daughter Suha to play school, Christine and I would go together on the metro to volunteer at Anna's House, a charitable institution serving meals to the needy. She was a true, selfless volunteer who would gladly do whatever she could to help the elderly with a hot meal. She also enthusiastically taught Korean to Swiss nationals from the Swiss Embassy. She was very active with church duty and had a large circle of friends, many of whom became my friends too, as she introduced me to them as her unni. She was excited to join the Diwali Ball organized by the ICCK and booked a table for 10 for her international friends, who attended draped in sarees with Indian jewellery, all borrowed from me.

She would not hesitate to pick up the phone and say, 'Unni, I want to eat dosa, I am coming to your place with Suha.' She would arrive, help herself to a beer can from the refrigerator and while savouring the dosa, we would continue to chat, ending our lunch with masala chai.

One day, I injured my finger while cutting vegetables as I was talking to her. She was horrified to see my finger bleed even as I coolly washed it, applied turmeric to the wound and the bleeding stopped. I told her the medicinal properties of turmeric and that we used it for all types of wounds. She was so impressed that she started telling all her Korean friends, popularizing our 'haldi' remedy. Once, she took my yoghurt 'culture' home to try and make it herself, and happily informed me that her husband liked the home-set yoghurt very much. It also took care of her husband's indigestion. Many other friends did the same and I was happy to learn that this home-made yoghurt helped their digestive systems. One of our Indian friends remarked jokingly, 'Sudha, you are really spreading Indian "culture" in Korea.'

Christine would bring friends to my place to taste Indian food, wear sarees and jewellery, take pictures and then post them on social media. Thanks to her wide network, I was able to host people from different countries, like Jiong from Canada, Giobana and Laura from Mexico, Regina from Argentina, Carolina from Chile, Myla from the Philippines, Elena from Russia, Angela from Columbia, and Kyunghee Park, Monica Park and Bock Hee Lee from Korea.

I still remember the fun we had at my place in November 2016 when Donald Trump was elected president of the US. Many international friends had come to my place to watch the election results being live-streamed on TV. Our friends were divided into two groups – for and against Trump. But more were for him, and there was cheering and celebration when he was declared the winner. Wine flowed freely, and my friends were surprised at the variety of Indian vegetarian dishes that I served.

Typical of Christine, she called me up one day and said, 'Unni, Regina is leaving Korea, when should I bring her and her South American friends to your place for the Indian experience? I will bring wine and a cake, and you prepare the rest.' Only Christine, my dear friend, could do this without any hesitation, and it was always a pleasure.

Christine had formed a group of five women called LIBAF, abbreviation of 'Life is beautiful with awesome friend'. The intention of the group was to travel together every year to different places, but with everyone's busy schedules, it did not happen. Instead, we met for coffee or lunch often and had a good time.

Even today, she sends pictures of little Suha's activities like skating, skiing, swimming and tennis, and of their trekking adventures. She wants Suha to join the Korean foreign service. I have given her the title 'super mom' after seeing her live six months in New Zealand for Suha's schooling, while Kevin continued to work in Korea. In 2023, when we went to Korea, it was such a delight to meet Christine and her family. I will never forget how Suha ran towards me and gave me a hug shouting 'Imo' when we went to see her in school.

I had lots of fun with Christine – visiting many places, meeting new friends, tasting Korean delicacies and makgeolli. When I was about to return to India, I asked her what she would like to have as a souvenir of our time together, and she picked up some of my steel utensils (engraved with my mother's best wishes in Marathi), saying that she will remember the dosa and Indian food she enjoyed at my place, and the good times we shared in Korea. She is now making plans to visit us in Mumbai where I look forward to hosting her.

In 2023, when my friend Kelly Yoon came to Mumbai with her husband for a business exhibition, we went out for dinner. It was Kelly's sixtieth birthday, which is as important a milestone in Korea as it is in India. In Korea, besides the first birthday celebrations (doljanchi) and the sixtieth birthday celebrations (hwangabjanchi), even the hundredth day after birth is a big occasion to celebrate (baeg-iljanchi). Kelly was overwhelmed when the restaurant people got a cake and candle, and the live band sang 'Happy Birthday' in English as well as in Korean. The restaurant staff were all K-drama buffs and got their pictures clicked with Kelly.

Like Kelly, Yoon Jinhee is another 'Bundango' friend who was always ready to help. I would call her my magic lamp genie. Even today, she's my ready reckoner if I need any information about Korea.

Coming back to my Japanese friend Keiko, who was instrumental in me joining Yeoksam Global Village Center and SIWA. 'You are Indian, right?' I heard a voice asking in English, and I turned around to find a slim, elegant lady – with looks like erstwhile Indian actress Nadira – looking at me with a smile. I was waiting for my cup of coffee during the Korean-class coffee break and replied, 'Yes, I am Indian.' I was glad to meet someone who knew English in my first month in Korea. 'I am Keiko, from Tokyo, studying at Level 3,' she said as she poured hot water in a box of noodles, with a cup of coffee in her other hand. She explained, 'I don't eat breakfast in the morning, so I have noodles now.'

I introduced myself by saying that I had recently arrived in Korea and was on Level 1. She seemed to be quite popular and friendly, and introduced her other friends to me. As my class was to resume after the break, she said, 'Wait after class. I will show you around Gangnam if you have time.' I happily agreed, and after class, we walked around the streets outside Gangnam station and went to a coffee shop. That is how the Keiko chapter of my life began!

As we were sipping coffee, I asked Keiko, 'Why did you come to Korea and learn Korean language?'

Keiko replied, 'You may be knowing the history that Japan once ruled Korea. They oppressed the Korean people a lot, forcing them to speak only the Japanese language and treating young Korean girls as "comfort women". After the end of World War II, Korea was free from Japanese rule, and after Korea's rapid economic development, Japanese boys and girls have been coming to Korea to learn the language, enjoy Korean cuisine and understand Korean culture better.

'I was an air hostess with an international airline and opted for voluntary retirement last year. I decided to come to Korea and live for a few months. After living here, I liked the friendly and helpful nature of Koreans, and also realized the bitterness Koreans harbour towards the Japanese, which is quite understandable given what they have gone through. I came last year and stayed for four months, rented a flat in Gangnam, attended Korean classes and worked as a volunteer at Anna's House. This year, I came last month and will be here for another two months. Now that I have met you, I would like to know more about your country.'

I was deeply touched by Keiko's explanation, her feeling of repentance for Japan's atrocities in Korea, and her wanting to learn Korean and do volunteer work here. Gradually, our friendship grew as we met regularly after class and bonded over coffee. I came to know about her family. Her husband, son and daughter-in-law were all doctors, and her daughter was studying in the US and planning to return to Japan to start a business. Since I was a vegetarian in my initial days in Korea, I could not eat out with her much but invited her to my place and introduced her to Indian vegetarian cuisine, which she thoroughly enjoyed. Whenever she came home, she would get me some goodies.

I remember, in December 2013, I was getting ready to go for my annual vacation to India (for the first time then), immediately after my birthday. Suddenly, the bell rang and there was Keiko, holding a cake and flowers with another Japanese friend carrying a bag with gifts for my family back in India! Then Keiko opened a bag and forced me to wear a kimono and take a picture, which I treasure even today. Keiko was truly generous and had a big heart; I called her my Japanese Santa Claus.

Keiko returned to Korea in September 2014, and we started meeting again regularly. She accompanied me to various places in Gangnam, about which I had to write in a monthly newsletter called *The Gangnam Gucheong News*, and happily posed for pictures. I went with her sometimes to a hospital to do volunteer work.

In August 2015, we went to Japan for a vacation and enjoyed Keiko's hospitality. She treated us to a sumptuous sushi lunch and showed us around. We were to meet soon in Korea in September, but she could not visit, as she was unwell and then had to go to the US for her daughter's graduation ceremony.

In 2016, I got an email from Keiko about her plans to visit India in December, when I would be there too. Her plan was to visit Delhi, Agra and Jaipur, and spend the last two days with me in Mumbai. I was really excited to host her in Mumbai! Closer to the date, I came to know that she was coming with a friend and, hence, would be staying at a hotel near the airport. I was surprised to get an email from Keiko asking for an appointment with a Bhrigu Samhita expert in Mumbai. I had heard of the Bhrigu Samhita as an ancient method of predicting one's future, but did not believe in astrology. After doing a Google search and asking some friends, I got some mobile numbers and contacted one expert near my house. I decided to go and see for myself before making an appointment for Keiko. The place turned out to be in an old, dilapidated building.

The Bhrigu Samhita is an ancient text written on palm leaves. An individual's palm leaf is traced from a stack of leaves by taking their left thumb impression. Questions are asked and palm leaves are passed over until the answer is correct. I tested some basic information, which turned out to be correct, and booked an appointment for Keiko. I was surprised to find out that this was free of cost and, fortunately, the expert could speak in English too to cater to a foreign client.

When I went to receive Keiko at the airport, after the excited greetings and hugs, the first thing Keiko's friend Yoshi said to me was, 'I want to see an elephant.' I was surprised that foreigners still think of India as a land of snake charmers with elephants on the streets. I replied patiently, 'For that, we can go to the zoo tomorrow. We will not find elephants on the streets.' As we got into the hired car and made our way to their hotel, we came across a wedding procession and lo and behold, what do we see? The groom on an elephant! Keiko and her friend were as excited as I was embarrassed because, just minutes before, I had told them you cannot find elephants on the streets. They happily clicked some pictures.

The next day, I took them to the Gateway of India, along the sea from Bandra Carter Road, via Sea Link, through Marine Drive. Keiko and her friend loved the drive; we had lunch at the Taj Mahal Palace Hotel and did some street shopping. On our return, we went to Juhu Beach and then did some serious gold jewellery shopping. I watched with amusement as Keiko was awestruck by the jewellery designs, and purchased quite a handful and flashed her credit card. The next day, I took her to the Bhrigu Samhita expert and, for two hours, Keiko's friend and I waited with bated breath outside, as she had gone in alone.

When she came out, she seemed visibly relieved and in good spirits. I did not ask her, neither did she say anything, but it did look like the mission had been accomplished. She was surprised that the expert refused to accept her envelope of cash. She came to my place, had her favourite dosas and as usual, my Santa Claus gave gifts to my mother, my cook and my domestic help. And then it was time to say goodbye. Once she reached Japan, she sent an email saying that she liked India and that she had added Mumbai to her list of favourite cities of the world, after Tokyo, London and Seoul.

There were fewer emails in 2017, and when Keiko came to Seoul in September with her daughter, she looked unwell. When we met for dinner a day before she was to leave, she opened up and said, 'Sudha, this will probably be my last visit to Seoul, as my cancer has spread. Tomorrow, I reach Tokyo and the chemotherapy treatment starts again.' I was speechless. After a pause, I managed to ask, 'Since when, Keiko?' She said, 'I came to know last year before coming to Mumbai when I had a surgery and the treatment started,' said Keiko.

She continued, 'I wanted to know from the Bhrigu Samhita expert whether I will be able to see a grandchild, and he said I will be able to see grandchildren. You know what, my daughter-in-law is due and going to have twins soon. The expert told me to be careful in 2018.' These were Keiko's last words as she got into the taxi and I bid her a tearful goodbye. I told her that I will pray for her health and would come to Tokyo in 2020 to watch the Olympic Games with her.

The year 2018 passed with some exchange of emails. In May that year, Keiko sent me pictures of her cute grandchildren. Her health was deteriorating, and she asked me to send emails even if she could not reply. In August 2019, we went to Japan for a short holiday and tried to contact Keiko but in vain. On my return, I got the news from a common friend that Keiko had passed away in late 2018 after seeing her grandchildren. The Bhrigu Samhita expert had been right, after all.

Keiko was the angel in my life who had introduced me to the Yeoksam Global Village Center and SIWA, which had enabled me to experience Korea to the fullest. For that, I will always be grateful.

I still had to find a way to make friends in my apartment complex. As I was beginning to learn the language, I thought to myself, 'Why don't I practise my Korean with my neighbours?' It started with greeting the receptionist in our apartment complex, then with some children and gradually with adults. I was the only Indian or, for that matter, foreigner, in our apartment building till then. Other people in the building had also heard about an Indian family coming to stay in the complex, and were curious to know more about me and my country. Gradually, I made a few friends in the apartment complex and introduced them to Indian cuisine and chai at my place.

Jin Myeong-wha would greet me with a smile as our paths crossed in the lobby. Once she came to know that I have learnt Korean, she invited me for a cup of coffee in the apartment cafeteria. There started a long, fruitful friendship with many luncheon meetings, sometimes with her daughter Na-young – who would happily drive us to fancy restaurants. I started calling her unni, and she introduced me to other neighbours as well. We continue to be in touch through social media and speak in Korean, and I appreciate her efforts to improve my Korean vocabulary with the use of appropriate words and by updating me with the local news. Friends like her motivate me to continue using Korean even today!

Sometimes, I wonder how friendship happens in the most unexpected situations. Once, Vasudev and I were out for a walk by the stream in the evening when a Korean couple passed us, and the lady smiled. I smiled back and she stopped. She introduced herself in English as Kim Hae-jong, and asked about me. She told me she taught English in a school and wanted some practice and, hence, started conversing with me. We exchanged phone numbers, and she invited us over for dinner to her place. This was the first time someone had invited us home for dinner rather than to eat out. Her husband worked as a senior official in a government department and was out of touch with English, which he had learnt many years ago while in the US. He, too, was glad to brush up his English-speaking skills with us. We became good friends and invited them to our place to taste Indian food. We are still in touch and met for dinner when we revisited Korea in 2023.

The fact that other Mahindra & Mahindra expat families stayed nearby was a great help, especially in the initial days. Rupa, Panchali, Maithili, Kanchan and Archana had already stayed in Korea for a couple of years, and shared their experiences with me. Vandana, Anjali, Neelima, Triveni, Radha and Shradha came later, over a period of time. Swati and Rupali came occasionally to Korea, as they continued to work in India. Many of the expats had children going to the international school and, hence, their routine was different from mine. Still, we had great fun together. We would meet for coffee at one of the three Starbucks near our apartment complex, or for lunch at one of the several restaurants on our Café Street. On some weekends, we would meet as families in some colleague's house, or go for a picnic or hike once a year. Every year, we celebrated the auspicious Gauri Ganapati festival at Vandana's place nearby and Tanuja's place in Jongno, and looked forward to the delicious traditional Maharashtrian dinner they cooked on the occasion.

In the last year of our stay, 2019, since one member had shifted back to India, I was inducted in the organizing committee of the Indians in Korea group. It was a wonderful experience to work with young, energetic Indians while organizing Ganapati and Diwali events.

As I was learning the language, I got some exciting opportunities to volunteer and make new friends.

Gangnam Publicity Ambassador

After about a year in Korea, having learnt basic Korean, I went with one of my friends to a meeting in downtown Seoul, which was supposed to be the mayor's open-house event. It had been arranged to listen to the voices of citizens and foreigners for improvement in governance. At the end, there was a Q&A session where I asked, 'If we don't have work visa but have experience in various fields, how can our services be utilized productively?' I did not expect a response, even though my question was duly noted along with my contact details.

After about 15 days, I got an email from the Gangnam administration office inviting me to an event. I was not sure whether I should go, since I didn't know what it was about. Nevertheless, I took two trains and went. I was in for a big surprise! The event was to discuss how to promote tourism in Gangnam, using the K-culture experience. Much to my surprise, I was appointed as a Gangnam publicity ambassador with no prior discussion. I guess this was their response to my question at the open house. A handful of other expats were also given similar certificates.

Afterwards, an official came up to me and explained, 'Sudha-ssi, remember that not only Gangnam, but the surrounding areas of Apgujeong, Garosu-gil, Apgujeong Rodeo Street, K-Star Road, Chong-dong, Sinsa-dong are your K-culture sections. You can walk around, take pictures and write articles about them in English. We will print them in our monthly newsletter *The Gangnam Gucheong News*. Even though our newsletter is in Korean, we plan to start carrying articles in English on the last page. This was our intention in appointing you as publicity ambassador. Good luck with your writing.'

After a sumptuous Korean lunch, we were taken in a bus to familiarize us with the tourist sites in and around Gangnam, including Cube Studios, famous for recording K-pop songs. We were asked to take pictures in front of K-pop stars' cut-outs, with flashy clothes and a mic in hand. To be honest, I had no idea of K-pop at the time. Walking along the famous K-Star Road and Apgujeong-Rodeo Street, we could see fashionable people shopping at the beauty product stores, and sipping coffee at upmarket restaurants along the street. The coordinator, who was showing us around, said, 'This is the fashion hub of Korea.'

At the tourism centre in Apgujeong, we were shown a presentation on K-beauty products as well as on cosmetic surgeries. The surgeries were said to be carried out in more than a thousand clinics in and around Gangnam. I was surprised and asked the coordinator, 'A thousand clinics? What is so special? I have not heard about these beauty-enhancing surgeries.' He replied, 'This is medical tourism. We are actively promoting it. Not just Koreans, many foreigners, especially from East Asia, are big fans of Korean films, series and K-pop stars, and want cosmetic surgery to look as beautiful as them. We have state-of-the-art facilities managed by skilled doctors, with easy access for patients to travel and have a comfortable stay.'

We were shown and given various types of tea to drink, containing herbs to combat stress, ageing and stomach ailments. The idea was to promote Korean health teas and ginseng in the international market. Later, we were shown shooting locations of many Korean dramas, such as Garosu-gil, Sinsa-dong and Chong-dong. While studying Korean, I only knew of a few series on YouTube. Now, I started thinking and understanding K-culture in a more in-depth way, since I had to write articles for the newsletter.

The first article I wrote was about the event that I had attended and the places they showed us on the first day of my appointment as the Gangnam publicity ambassador. It was printed in the December 2014 issue of *The Gangnam Gucheong News*. I got a message that my article was published, along with a request for my bank account details. Within two days, I got a credit in my bank account. It was an honorarium for the article, and though it was a modest sum, I was thrilled! I informed them that I did not have a work visa but they assured me that they were a government organization and that a small honorarium was permissible.

I started getting invitations for events in and around Gangnam, which I attended and wrote about for the newsletter. Once, I got a call at 2 p.m. from the newsletter's office, asking me to submit an article by 5 p.m. on Dosan Garden, which had become famous during the Korean independence struggle. As it turned out, I was having lunch at a Turkish restaurant in Gangnam with an Indian friend, Panchali, who was returning to India in a few days after having lived in Korea for four years. I said yes to the assignment, and asked Panchali if she would like to join me. She agreed, and after a hasty lunch, we took a taxi to Dosan Garden in Apgujeong.

We walked around the historic garden, gathered information, took pictures and returned home by train. I quickly compiled the information and photos, and submitted the article two minutes before 5 p.m. Panchali, who was watching me curiously, said, 'Sudha, Korean efficiency has rubbed off on you within a year.' I told her, 'Since I don't have a work visa, I want to make the most of whatever opportunity I get.'

The next assignment I got was as a food and sanitation inspector at Gangnam. The health and sanitation department had started a new initiative by appointing some foreigners to conduct inspections of restaurants. This was a novel idea, since the restaurant staff did not expect foreigners to do government inspection work. I was allowed to take another person with me instead of going alone, to make my visit appear authentic.

Over the next three months, I covered about 20 restaurants in Gangnam with either Vasudev or one of my friends. My role was to observe the hygiene level, the quality of the food served and the way the staff treated customers, especially foreigners. I then had to submit a report written in Korean to the sanitation department. I went to various Korean, Japanese, Thai, Vietnamese, Turkish, Italian and Indian restaurants, and at none of these places did the staff suspect that I was an inspector! In most cases, all the standards were met, and in some cases, where deficiency was reported, I understand that action was initiated.

This was an enriching experience for me, where I could try out different cuisines and received an honorarium for it too. It was quite an interesting way for Korean authorities to utilize the services of foreigners who did not have a work visa.

Seoul Namdaemun Police

Language is an issue for foreigners in Korea. The authorities are aware of it and try to take steps to make life easier for them. This was part of the reason why the Seoul Namdaemun Police appointed a few foreigners as volunteers. Due to my activities in Gangnam, somebody I had met recommended my name as a police volunteer with Seoul Namdaemun Police, since I had become fairly proficient in Korean by then.

The purpose of having foreigners as police volunteers was to overcome the language barrier, understand the cultural differences and to help foreigners navigate life in Korea with greater confidence. I started attending meetings at the Seoul Namdaemun Police Station, where they briefed us volunteers about Korean laws as well as the issues foreigners face and how to resolve them. These fortnightly meetings in Korean were followed by a team dinner, where I got to know my colleagues and the cases they had worked on.

I had the privilege to witness the signing of an important MoU between Seoul police and a reputed law firm, which was a landmark scheme for the safety of foreign nationals. I was the only foreigner in this meeting. I was wearing a saree and was introduced as an Indian; people looked at me curiously.

I would often get calls from the police headquarters to deal with the problems of foreign citizens. These included domestic disputes between non-Korean women and their Korean husbands, often caused by cultural differences. These were reported to the police department either directly or through lawyers or respective embassies. Many such issues were resolved with counselling, which gave me a lot of personal satisfaction.

The police department had created a commendable campaign called 'Make a Wish', aimed at senior citizens living solitary lives. They were asked to make a wish and the police department would fulfil that wish, if it was possible to do so. An elderly woman who lived alone was fond of watching TV series. She expressed a wish to a police volunteer that she wanted to watch her favourite actors on a bigger screen. I went with our team to her house and we installed a big Samsung TV, much to her delight. I was touched to see her in tears that her wish for a big TV had come true, and that she could now watch her favourite actor, Lee Min-ho, clearly. She then noticed me, and seeing my Indian dress, she started feeling the fabric and my ornaments, and was curious to know about India. We soon became friendly.

Another unforgettable incident was when we visited a very senior citizen, born in 1930, who lived in a small, ancient house up a hill in Seoul. When one of our police volunteers asked him to make a wish, he mentioned his desire to try new medicinal tonics.

I trudged along with my team members up the steep slope, carrying a box of tonics and household articles, and reached his place only to find that he had gone down to fetch a newspaper. Since the house was open, we peeped inside. The tiny house was filled with old gadgets and newspapers. What struck me was how well-maintained everything looked, despite the fact that the space wasn't large and everything was quite old. Soon, the 88-year-old gentleman came walking with sprightly steps, up the same slope that had left us huffing and puffing. He was surprised to see us waiting.

When he got to know the purpose of our visit, he was quite surprised and said, 'I had only mentioned the tonics but I had not asked for them. You have misunderstood. I get government pension and free medical treatment. Please give these tonics to an elderly person who really needs them instead of me. I have bequeathed my property to go to the nation after my death. I do not need any help from my country. Please take this back and give to someone else or to a charitable organization.' Saying this, he bowed and went into his house.

I admired his self-respect and love for his country, and did not want to leave without speaking to him. I entered his house and said, 'Uncle, you are my father's age. I have come all the way from India. I would like to have a chat, a cup of tea and take a picture with you.' The gentleman did not disappoint us and came down the hill with our team, had a cup of tea with us and posed for a picture.

During our conversation, I came to know that he had been a newspaper editor, was well read and knew quite a few things about India, like the Taj Mahal and places like Bodhgaya and Ayodhya. We also spoke about India's development and democracy. Later, we bid goodbye and saw him climb back up the hill to his house.

Once, I got the opportunity to go to the border dividing North and South Korea with my police colleagues. I had been there quite a few times with Indian guests, but this time it was different, since I was attending an event covered by media. A Korean TV journalist asked me my opinion as an Indian citizen, and I said in Korean, 'Any division is terrible and we are seeing its consequences. I hope both Koreas will be united someday.' I was in India when this was shown on TV, and one of my Korean friends had been kind enough to send me a video clip of my moment of fame.

The seventy-fourth anniversary ceremony of the Korean National Police was held in Incheon in October 2019, where I was invited along with my police colleagues. This was a major event attended by senior police officials from different parts of Korea. We were accommodated in a five-star hotel, where we had a rehearsal of the event followed by a lavish dinner. While others enjoyed Korean delicacies like bulgogi, the organizers were considerate enough to serve vegetarian food for me. The next day, we had to sing the police anthem in front of distinguished dignitaries. People were surprised to see a saree-clad Indian singing in Korean in front of TV cameras. Later, at lunch with senior police officials, many were curious about my attire and wanted to be photographed with me. My day was made!

Before we left Korea in December 2019, I was invited to the annual police party with Vasudev, which also happened to be on my birthday. And what a surprise it was for me! They arranged for a cake-cutting programme and sang the Korean birthday song. A video presentation was made with highlights from my volunteer work with the police. Since I was going to leave Korea, they gave me a trophy and a certificate, which I will cherish forever. I was asked to give a speech, which turned out to be my first and last speech in Korean!

I had promised myself when learning Korean that I should be able to give a farewell speech in Korean when it was time to leave. I was glad I could do it. I had had dinner on many occasions with my police colleagues but had never gone out with them for a second round of drinks. After the event and dinner, since Vasudev was with me, my police friends insisted we go out with them for a second round, and were very happy when we joined them. Our driver, who also attended this event, remarked solemnly as we were leaving, 'Ma'am, you came to Korea as a foreigner ('oegug-saram'), and today, you have truly become one of us ('hangug-saram').' I was deeply moved.

Volunteering with the police helped me understand Korean society more closely, as I got to meet different kinds of people and make wonderful friends. During our 2023 trip to Seoul, I went to the Seoul Namdaemun Police Station to meet some colleagues. Many had been transferred, and the person at the reception connected me on phone with one friend who then asked me to wait. Vasudev and I waited for about 20 minutes and thought of leaving, assuming that she must be busy. To our surprise, she arrived to see me. She had also been transferred to another police station nearby but had picked up a gift, taken a taxi and come to meet me.

'Serving' at Anna's House

Thanks to my friends in SIWA, I got an opportunity to help at a social service organization called Anna's House (Ana-ae Jib). It provides free evening meals to more than 600 people on an average every day. Typically, the beneficiaries were the destitute, homeless, disabled, elderly or sick. Volunteers like me helped wash the vegetables, which were donated by well-wishers, and cut them. After the meal was cooked, we served the 600 people, cleaned up the place and washed the dishes. Most volunteers had their meal after all the activity was completed, but I preferred to eat at home.

Volunteers were from various walks of life – foreigners like me, people from the corporate world doing CSR (corporate social responsibility) activity, college students, homemakers, devout Christians and representatives of churches, and sometimes, even celebrities.

Every Wednesday, at 4 p.m., I would go to Anna's House to assist in preparing the evening meal. The rule was to fill one's plate only once. I enjoyed serving the elderly, many times getting a request for more kimchi or rice, since they could take only once. I felt blessed to see the smile on their grateful faces. It was so satisfying to see them off after a hearty meal as they boarded the bus organized to take them home.

Anna's House was initially started in 1998 as an evangelical activity by Father Vincenzo Bordo, an Italian missionary. In 1998–99, during the financial crisis, many small businesses collapsed and several people lost their jobs. This is when Anna's House started serving one meal a day at their soup kitchen to people in need and saved many from starvation. This practice continues even today, after nearly 25 years, since there are still hungry and needy people despite Korea's economic prosperity.

All the ingredients required for cooking at such a large scale regularly are received by way of donations from charitable organizations, big companies and affluent families. Over the years, this initiative became very popular and the Korean government recognized the humanitarian service rendered by Father Vincenzo Bordo by awarding him Korean citizenship and a Korean name, Kim Ha-jong.

Father Vincenzo started another initiative to care for adolescent orphans, providing them education to be future-ready. Once, on 15 August, Korea's Independence Day as well as India's, he invited me and Vasudev to talk to the adolescents about India, followed by a Q&A session with them. The interaction ended with an Indian lunch that we had organized with the help of our friend, Shyam Paliwal, owner of the Indian restaurant chain Bombay Brau.

I found Father Vincenzo to be a simple, straightforward person. After his morning prayers, he spends his entire day doing chores at Anna's House. His enthusiasm is infectious, and his ever-smiling face motivated me and all the other volunteers to serve wholeheartedly at Anna's House.

During the Covid-19 crisis, since people could not come to the soup kitchen, food packets were arranged to be sent to them, along with water bottles and face masks. Seeing these pictures on social media brought a smile on my face.

Korea Dyslexia Association

A friend in SIWA introduced me to Shin Young-hwa, who had started the Korea Dyslexia Association (Dehanmingug Nandogchung) as a support group for students with learning disabilities and their parents. Since I had worked with children with special needs in India, I thought I could add value to the Association's efforts.

I started going to the Korea Dyslexia Association twice a week to volunteer. I worked with school students who had dyscalculia (the inability to grasp numbers and mathematical concepts) of Grades 8, 9 and 10. Since my Korean and their mathematics were at a similar level, we learnt by helping each other. My Korean improved, as did their mathematics. I learnt Korean words for 'point', 'line' and 'triangle', right up to 'Pythagoras theorem', and also taught them some tricks in trigonometry.

I tried to instil an element of fun while teaching mathematics, which I had learnt from my father, Prof. M.S. Huzurbazar, a renowned professor of mathematics. It was a great feeling to get positive feedback from students as well as parents. I realized that language need not be an issue while teaching mathematics. Love, trust, simplifying mathematical concepts that are universal and focussing on students' strengths – everything I would incorporate while teaching students with dyscalculia in Mumbai were effective in Korea too!

The mood in the classroom was usually upbeat, with a lot of chatter about what had happened in school, and students helping each other with mathematical problems. I would chip in with stories about India, and as I was still learning Korean, the students would at times have a good laugh and correct my language. When the parents came to pick up the children, invariably the students would ask me to extend the session to solve more problems. The real reason, I am sure, was that they enjoyed the company of their friends. Of course, the parents would not complain and waited happily, seeing this positive change in their children.

I continued for about three years, but then the lease of the premises expired and the Association shifted to a place that was two hours from where I lived. Reluctantly, I bid the students and their parents goodbye. I was touched when the parents arranged a farewell party for me and gave me precious mementos!

The Korea Dyslexia Association has made a video on YouTube with a collage of my pictures taken during my three-year stint, saying, 'Gamsahamnida, Sudha Imo.' Some parents are still in touch with me on social media. On 15 May, which is Korean Teachers' Day, I still get greetings from some of the parents on KakaoTalk. Most of the students would have grown up by now, and passed college too. I hope, somewhere, at the back of their minds, there will be a memory of an Indian teacher who taught them how to have fun with numbers.

Having worked in the field of people with different kind of disabilities in India, I tried to understand the system in Korea for people with disabilities. The infrastructure in Korea is by and large disability-friendly, with ramps at appropriate places. There are braille notifications at public places, traffic signals and even in apartment elevators. Traffic signals also have sound notifications for the visually impaired. I learnt that, in school, they have an 'inclusive' education system where children with disabilities are in the same class as other children, and teachers and helpers are able to manage a class of 20–25 students. There are also parent support groups, and institutions that provide vocational training to the students after they turn 16.

I came across quite a few young parents who had returned after staying abroad for the sake of their children with special needs. These were highly qualified people who chose to return so that their children could learn the mother tongue at an early age, attend Korean school and also get family support. Some came to our house to seek advice, and I was touched to see the children eating and playing in our house, oblivious to what was happening around them, even as their parents shared their worries about the future.

Learning Korean helped me make many friends ('chingu') and do volunteer work. Korean language was the key with which I could unlock a treasure of valuable experiences. I am still in touch with my Korean friends on KakaoTalk, and it is a pleasure to see see them upload our pictures on social media, with captions saying, 'Unni, we miss you. When are you coming back?'

6

Travel in Four Seasons

Before going to Korea, we had only heard about four seasons, never experienced them. The best months in Korea for us were in spring, approximately from April to mid-June, and in autumn, approximately from mid-September to November, when the temperatures ranged from 10–25 degrees Celsius. Koreans love winters too, but as Indians from Mumbai we are used to mild or non-existent winters. We were not comfortable in the harsh Korean winter, where the temperature ranges from -1 to -15 degrees Celsius. Koreans do not like summer, which ranges from mid-June to August, when the maximum temperature can go up to 35–38 degrees Celsius; summer also brings rains.

Spring

Spring brought a spring in our step after having to stay indoors all winter. Come late March or early April, it is cherry-blossom season. The flower is called 'beojkkoch' in Korean and 'sakura' in Japanese. Cherry blossoms last only for a week and different places may see it bloom at different times, so the entire season might range from 15–20 days overall in Korea. But what a sight it is while it lasts!

The white-pink trees are a sight to behold. One does not find them everywhere; there are only a few places famous for cherry blossoms where people throng during those few days and click pictures as if there is no tomorrow. Once the trees bloom, within a week, it becomes windy and rains, resulting in the withering of flowers that form a white carpet on the ground, which is also appealing to the eye against the green backdrop.

In the first year of our stay in Korea, we went to a place about 350 km south of Seoul called Jinhae that our Korean friends had recommended for its cherry-blossom season. There were streets lined with cherry trees in full bloom, and while walking down, we could not see the sky thanks to the white-pink canopy created by the cherry trees. Lot of tourists like us were there to experience this short-lived miracle of beauty. Since it was our first time, we immensely enjoyed it, and returned home the same night; not exhausted but excited about what we had just seen.

The next morning, we went down to find cherry trees in full bloom outside our apartment complex. Of course, this was a mini version of what we had seen at Jinhae, but still, they were cherry blossoms and were so close to us. Till then, we had no clue that the trees on our street were cherry trees. I remarked to Vasudev jokingly about why we had travelled 350 km to witness cherry blossoms when they were at our doorstep! But of course, Jinhae was special with its long line of cherry trees on various streets, and it was definitely worth the drive.

Every year, we visited different places for cherry-blossom season – like Gimhae, Chuncheon and Hadong – and if we couldn't travel far, we would go to Yeouido in Seoul. Wherever we went, there would be a fair-like atmosphere with people, both locals and tourists, revelling in that fairy-tale, white-pink world. Perhaps people value it so much because it is so short.

Before going to Korea, we had heard about sakura in Japan from Indian tourists, since there were special tours from India to Japan around that time. Even then, we heard stories that not everyone is lucky enough to witness cherry blossoms, since the days might vary from year to year. But we were not aware of the cherry-blossom season in Korea. We realized there were more locals than foreign tourists at the places we went to in Korea. We had gone to Japan but not in the sakura season. We also came to know of cherry-blossom season in other parts of the world, like Michigan and Melbourne, and were surprised to see some white-blooming cherry trees along the Eastern Express Highway in Mumbai too.

In spring, perhaps to coincide with cherry-blossom season, white and pink are popular colours for dresses, scarves, purses and accessories. I am not sure if everyone in Korea does it, but my friends told me they changed their wardrobe every year – donating their old clothes and shopping for new. After all, one should not be seen in the same dress in the pictures every year. So much for sustainability!

Come spring, and it was time for Vasudev to hit the golf course after the winter break. Many of our family members and friends visited us in either spring or autumn. Some of our friends were non-vegetarian, in which case we took them out to have a taste of Korean cuisine. But in most cases, our relatives and friends were vegetarians. I had to pack our meals while going out, and cook vegetarian dinner at home after returning from sightseeing and shopping. At times, we managed to treat them in a vegan restaurant.

We had some memorable trips with our son Chinmay and his family. They visited us often in the month of May, away from the sweltering heat in India, after their return from Italy. We once went to Busan, the second biggest city in Korea, known for its beach and seafood, especially sashimi and octopus delicacies. The super-fast KTX train takes you from Seoul to Busan in less than two-and-a-half hours. Vasudev had used it once for official work. But we liked to go by car, so that we could see more places along the way.

When we were driving to Busan, we took a slight detour that took us to Gyeongju – a World Heritage site known for its ancient Buddhist temple, art by way of sculptures, pagodas and big, green mounds that are the royal tombs of the kings and queens from the ancient Silla Kingdom.

As we were nearing Busan, our driver Jay got a call from his uncle who stayed there. After their conversation was over, I asked Jay why he was fighting with his uncle. He laughed and clarified, 'We were not fighting. The Busan dialect is different, it sounds a bit harsh.'

The next day was the Buddha's birthday, and we visited a temple in Busan. Most of the temples are on hill tops, offering a panoramic view, and in Busan, it was an ocean view. It was a wonderful sight, with colourful paper lanterns forming a canopy all along the path to the temple. There was a big crowd because of the special occasion, but what made the deepest impression on us were how patiently and quietly people moved in a queue, and the cleanliness all around. There were no offerings of flowers but only placing of incense sticks at a designated place. After the temple visit, we went to our friend Shyam's Indian restaurant, Bombay Brau, for a delicious lunch. Our grandson Siddhartha, who had had enough of temples, remarked with a sigh, 'Thank god. No more temples.' Shyam then showed us his brewery and explained the process, which was quite interesting. More interesting was tasting the beer.

Namhae is the southern-most tip of Korea, known for its picturesque drive. The view was gorgeous, with sea water all around and houses with colourful roofs adorning the village. It is famous for anchovy ('myolchi' in Korean), and Koreans drive all the way to Namhae to enjoy this seafood. We enjoyed our seafood lunch in a restaurant that was on a cliff with a breathtaking view; pleasant breeze blew on our faces. We then went down to the beach and had a great time opening our newly purchased tent, which little Siddhartha later insisted be opened in our living room for the rest of his vacation.

On our way back, Jay recommended that we have a look at the German village nearby. I was curious and asked Jay, 'German? What is so special to have a German village?'

He explained that Namhae County developed this village and had given subsidies to Koreans who had gone to work in Germany as migrant workers, to earn foreign exchange, so that they could settle there upon their return. Many Koreans worked all their lives in Germany and returned to Korea after retirement. Some married there, and returned with their German spouses and culture.

It was no surprise to see many structures having European or German look in that village. Neat, colourful houses lined on either side of the street. There were pubs, restaurants and coffee shops as well. Needless to say, the first thing Vasudev did was go to the pub and have German beer. While sipping beer, we came to know from the bartender that this village also celebrates Oktoberfest, like they do in Munich, which attracts thousands of tourists there. Even at other times, this place has become a tourist attraction, which is why Jay had taken us there.

We headed back home, which was to be a four-hour drive. On the drive back, for the sake of conversation, I mentioned to seven-year-old Siddhartha that Jay stays all alone in Korea, whereas his family, including his parents and brothers, live in the US. I was expecting some sympathy from Siddhartha towards Jay but he asked him immediately, 'Jay Uncle, do you have first cousin in Korea?' Jay said, 'Yes, I have many.' Siddhartha replied, 'You are lucky, I don't have any.' It took Vasudev and me some time to understand the depth of our grandson's statement. When a child does not have a sibling, they may feel lonely. With Chinmay and Divya both being single children, it never crossed our minds that their son will not even have a first cousin. I was surprised that a seven-year-old child had this in his mind, and that it came out spontaneously.

Summer

After mid-June, it starts getting hot, and July and August are the hottest months, accompanied by rains. After being used to heavy rains in Mumbai, we found the rains in Korea quite mild. Very rarely did we have downpours throughout the day. Occasional heavy showers are easy to manage for people as well as the administrators.

During our stay, we did not experience any disruption due to rain, but Jay told us that just a fortnight before we reached Korea in 2013, it had rained so heavily that buses had been submerged in parking lots and there had been widespread transport disruption. Warning messages will flash on your mobile phones if it is likely to rain heavily or if the temperatures are expected to rise beyond a certain point, advising citizens to take precautions, drink water and avoid certain places like the riverside.

Since we are used to hotter summers in India and heavier rains, we were able to cope better with the summer than the Koreans. In the absence of ceiling fans, air conditioners are used continuously in summer. We had some pedestal fans in our house, which we used occasionally. My friends would want the air conditioner on and a chilled drink as soon as they entered our house in summer. During this season, iced tea and cold coffee are the common drinks, besides chilled beer.

The dresses and fashion change accordingly. Cottons and shorts are common casual clothes outside office.

Whenever I travelled back to Korea from India, I would carry a variety of cotton dresses and scarves to gift my Korean friends. They loved the vibrant colours of Indian dresses, so much so that summers and autumn became a celebration of Indian clothes in Korea for my friends.

We were fortunate to be in Korea in the summer of 2014 to watch the Asian Games in Incheon. It was the first time we were watching a track and field event; we enjoyed it thoroughly. We got to see some table tennis games, Indian star P.V. Sindhu's badminton match and Sania Mirza in action in the mixed-doubles finals that India won.

We were one of the few cheering for the Indians shouting, 'India! India!' The majority were Koreans shouting 'Daehan Minguk' followed by three claps, which was quite rhythmic.

Vasudev's only regret was his inability to go to the India–Pakistan hockey finals with his friends. It turned out to be an exciting game, with India winning in the shootout. He was a silent spectator as his friends discussed the match for the next 10 days.

Later, we got a chance to see P.V. Sindhu again in action in a badminton tournament and also got to meet the Indian women's hockey team when they were in Seoul. In India, we take things for granted and are content watching games on TV, but outside the country, it is a different feeling to cheer on Indian sportspersons.

We got an opportunity to visit Jeonju, famous for bibimbap, when the ICCK organized a trip there to play golf. We drove down to find a quaint, charming town with hanoks. This place is a tourist attraction, with hanoks available as homestays. We did not stay but were fortunate to witness a festival of lotus flowers followed by an authentic bibimbap lunch.

School and college students have their summer vacation in July and August. Even SsangYong would be closed for a week for summer vacation and annual maintenance in the first week of August. This is the time when everybody seems to travel, both within and outside Korea. Various places in Korea organize different festivals to attract tourists. We went to Taean for a tulip festival, similar to what we see in the Netherlands, and to Boryeong where they have a mud festival like the 'tomatina' festival in Spain (as depicted in the Hindi movie *Zindagi Na Milegi Dobara*) or, for that matter, like Holi, our festival of colours. The mud here is considered rich in minerals and is used in the manufacture of cosmetics. The mud festival was conceived as a marketing tool for Boryeong mud cosmetics and today it attracts thousands of tourists in summer.

Thanks to the one-week summer vacation Vasudev got in August, and a few days in September for Chuseok, we were able to plan foreign travel better from Korea. Koreans do not need a tourist visa for most countries except India. We wanted to go to the US for the first time, and dreaded the visa procedure after listening to the woes of our friends back in India. After filling out the forms, we went to the US Embassy in Seoul and were in for a surprise. There was hardly anyone in the Embassy. Our forms were accepted over casual conversation and we were out in 30 minutes. Our passports were couriered within two days, and we got our US visa for 10 years without a sweat! We found obtaining a visa from concerned embassies was much easier than what we experienced in India.

Our Korean friends would always wonder why we required a visa to go to any country, as they would just fly out with their passport. Our first trip outside Korea was to Vietnam. We planned it because my Indian friend said that visa was not required for Vietnam. Later, we came to know that visa was required for Indians; my friend who had told me was a US resident. We had to scramble and got our visa just a day before departure.

We had some anxious moments while going to Serbia. Vasudev had read that Indians do not require a visa to go to Serbia. He booked the flight to Belgrade happily. When we reached Incheon airport, for a moment, my heart was in my mouth when the check-in counter staff told us we cannot leave Korea, since we do not have a visa to go to Serbia. She had assumed that Indians require a visa to go to any country. After showing the rules that visa is not required for Indians to go to Serbia, and pleading in Korean, she called her senior, who fortunately checked the rules and allowed us to go. Ah, what a relief!

Wherever we travelled across the globe, we used to bump into some Koreans, either at the airport or some tourist spot clicking pictures. Since I knew their language, I could understand what they were saying. Not in their wildest dreams would they imagine that an Indian will understand what they were saying. I used to derive immense pleasure in surprising them by greeting in Korean saying 'annyeonghaseyo', and they would get startled. I would then continue to speak in Korean and click their pictures, and more than once, met people who stayed near my apartment in Seoul.

Once, when we were in Mongolia, we were searching for a temple and had some issue with the GPS. We asked some people on the road, but language was an issue, since they did not understand English. We went to a souvenir shop, looked around and asked the owner in English for the directions to the temple. The result was the same – she did not understand English. I was so frustrated that I exclaimed my helplessness by saying something in Korean. The lady was shocked and excited. 'Hanguk?' she asked me. I nodded. This lady was a North Korean, and she was so happy to converse in Korean that she came out of the shop and guided us halfway to the temple. I realized then how knowing a language can come to your aid in difficult situations.

While living in Korea, there was a tendency to compare the various countries we visited with Korea. We always came back saying that Korea is better in terms of public transport system, safety, infrastructure, cleanliness and general ease of living. I always felt that if we were to go to these countries from India, we would have been more generous in our perception while comparing them with India. Even though we travelled in the peak seasons of summer and Chuseok vacation, when the airports were packed with people, it was still a smooth check-in process, (albeit standing in long, disciplined queues) and getting out of the airport on our return was always quick and efficient.

After Chuseok, autumn sets in.

Autumn

Autumn brings with it a riot of colours, known as 'danpung' (fall colours of maple leaves), when the trees and plants change hues as temperatures drop. There is a touch of yellow and orange to the green foliage, which looks stunning.

People throng to national parks during autumn to appreciate the beauty of nature, while wearing clothes that match the fall colours. Just like during the cherry-blossom season, there is a festive atmosphere for people to celebrate autumn at national parks.

Nami Island, about 70 km from our house, was where we liked to take our guests to admire the scenic beauty. You have to take a ferry to reach the island where no vehicles are allowed. Else, you can zip across on the zip-line. Our guests liked the theme of this island where ferry tickets are termed as 'visas', as if you are going to another country. Once you reach the island, a big board with the words 'Nami Nara' welcomes you, and you can find flags of different nations. There are interesting games and activities for children, good places to eat, a well-stocked library and even some cottages facing the water to stay in (which have to be booked in advance). On the way back, Jay would take a detour to show our guests a nice garden called 'Garden of Morning Calm' in late evening, where they could witness dazzling lights adorning the different trees and bushes. Sometimes, he would take them to Petite France, a cute replica of a French village close to the Garden of Morning Calm.

Another scenic place that we took our guests to was Seoraksan National Park, where there are a grand Buddha statue and a cable car ride as attractions. Jeju island was our favourite destination. We visited it in all seasons except winter, but more than once during autumn to witness the fall colours.

Koreans have a saying that one has not seen Korea if one has not visited Jeju Island. It is a very popular tourist place for the locals as well as foreigners, which one can reach only by air or sea transport. The volcanic terrain lends itself to lot of outdoor adventures. There are mountains to explore (like the Hallasan), black-sand beaches, waterfalls, lakes, caves and lava tubes formed by volcanic eruptions. The government has developed this place for tourism with lots of activities and incentives, so much so that tourists from some countries do not require a visa if they visit only Jeju.

There are many museums like trick-eye museum, auto museum, sex and health museum, glass museum, teddy bear museum, and many other theme-based ones for all age-groups. We enjoyed a trek to Hallasan; had a submarine ride; visited interesting parks, caves and museums; and most importantly, enjoyed the Korean cuisine and the famous Jeju oranges and cactus chocolates. We were told that barbequed black boar was a local delicacy.

While in Jeju, we took a trip to Udo Island, where we enjoyed their famous peanut ice cream. We also learnt some history about 'haenyo', women divers who used to go deep into the sea to harvest seaweed, shellfish and abalone. In the past, when there were no oxygen cylinders, these women did this work by holding their breath as much as possible. They would be exposed to great risks and extreme cold, and many lost their lives in accidents. Nowadays, these women divers are equipped with oxygen tanks and warm clothing, and are covered by insurance. I later got to read Lisa See's book *The Island of Sea Women* that dealt with the lives of the women divers; it was very touching.

Appreciating fall colours was a new experience for us. I remember Vasudev telling me when he had returned from China in December 2012 that he did not like the place because it seemed so barren; he could not see many leaves or much greenery where he had been. This was because his visit had been in winter and, till we moved to Korea, we had never experienced the transition from autumn to winter. In Korea, we realized for the first time that in winter, the trees indeed do look barren.

Winter

Towards the second half of November, the temperature dips to single digits, and by December it is at zero or below. It would be time for me to pack for my annual trip to India like a migratory bird. I can withstand hot summers, but cannot bear the cold winds blowing on my face. We were comfortable inside the house with centrally heated rooms, but for how long can one be cocooned? Vasudev would go in his car to office comfortably, but I had to take public transport if I had to go out and hence had to face the elements.

Before going on my annual winter vacation to India, I would cook some things for Vasudev for the next three months, and he would get some 'methi theplas' from India.

In Korea, there is a nice system of providing a huge deep freezer in the kitchen. It was in the form of deep drawers called 'kimchi trays', with temperatures ranging from −6 to −36 degrees Celsius. This is used by Koreans to preserve fish, kimchi and vegetables that are not easily available during winter.

We stored groceries and snacks we got from India in them, and things I cooked before my India trips would remain quite fresh in the freezer even after months. It used to be a surprise to our Indian guests when we could serve them sev puri, aam ras and maghai paan fresh from the deep freezer. Recently, one of our friends in India, Vinita, who had been to our house in Korea, fondly remembered the kimchi tray and the pav bhaji that she had eaten after a tiring day at the DMZ.

It does not snow very often in Korea, maybe about 10 to 15 times in the four months of winter. Due to pollution and climate change, my friends say the snowfall has declined in recent years. Many times, the temperature is less than −5 degrees Celsius and at times, less than −10 degrees Celsius. Winters in Korea are deceptive because during the day, it is very bright with a clear blue sky, unlike in Europe where days are dull and gloomy in winter. And if there is a breeze, which there often is, it is bone-chilling.

I learnt from my Korean friends to dress appropriately in winter, especially to cover my neck and protect my feet with heat pads inside shoes. Of course, it was only for early December and late March; during the rest of the winter months, I was in Mumbai. I covered myself from head to toe and layered up: first the thermal wear, then two or three layers of woollen clothes, heat pads in shoes and on my back, scarf to cover my neck and face, and a cap and gloves. I was not bothered when my friend made fun of me for being overdressed. During winter, the smell of hot coffee and baked goods is everywhere in the air, and the urge to drink coffee comes unknowingly. With hot coffee, having something sweet like cakes, cookies or buns adds to the fun.

Vasudev was cautioned by his friends repeatedly to wear shoes with a firm grip, and to walk carefully to avoid slipping on roads when it snows. As I was in India most of the winter, he would tell me how impressed he was with the accuracy of weather forecasts of snowfall. Many times, there would be no tell-tale signs, then the weather would turn suddenly and it would snow, just as the forecast had predicted! During winter, Vasudev's favourite activities were indoors and with his friends like bowling, baseball, playing golf on a simulator or occasional visits to a karaoke bar.

In Korea, most of my Korean friends maintain a central temperature of 16 degrees Celsius in their homes. The temperature in our house would be set at 23 degrees Celsius. At first, it was 25 degrees Celsius, but once my Korean neighbour said, 'It's too hot, turn on the fan.' I then set the temperature to 23 degrees Celsius but never went below that. I did not want to sit in the house wearing a sweater.

Snowfall is managed very well by the administration. It uses blowers to clear snow regularly from the roads. I did not experience any flight cancellation while going to Mumbai in December after the first snowfall. Once, there was heavy snowfall in the morning and the snow covered everything – trees, vehicles, houses and roads. I was wondering whether my flight would be cancelled. My friend messaged me, 'Safe travels.' I expressed my concern that the flight may not take off and that I may have to return from the airport. She replied confidently, 'Don't worry. Your flight will not be cancelled. At the most, there could be a delay of one or two hours to clear the snow from the runway.' She was right! I managed to reach the airport on time and after a two-hour delay, during which I saw workers using heavy machinery to clear the snow, the plane took off and reached Mumbai only an hour behind schedule.

Koreans love winter. Indeed, the air seems fresher and people welcome the snowfall by flocking to ski resorts. We would see children near our house playing in the snow, throwing snow balls at each other, giggling, happy. While we never went to a ski resort, we saw videos of friends with their children seated in snow tubes, and parents pushing them gently down the slopes. Some of our friends travelled to Hokkaido in north Japan, which is famous for its ski resorts and scenic beauty.

Life in winter carries on, with most houses, offices, restaurants, shops, malls, vehicles and public transport well heated. For people who use public transport, underground metro stations with their shops and restaurants are a safe haven. Those using cars go from the underground parking area of their apartments to similar ones at malls and offices without having to brave the cold weather.

When I was in Mumbai in the winter of 2017–18, Vasudev got a chance to go to Pyeongchang to witness the Winter Olympics in February 2018 with his company's senior leadership team. He says it was an experience of a lifetime!

The temperature was around −5 degrees Celsius, Vasudev was fully covered and was still freezing. There, out in the cold, he was amazed to see athletes skiing, manoeuvring themselves with great skill as they competed in the world's most prestigious winter sports competition. He was also excited to see ice hockey and figure skating, and learnt of a new sport called 'luge'. He treasures the muffler, cap and gloves with the Pyeongchang Olympics logo that he got as a souvenir. Whenever I see them in Mumbai, I break out in a sweat!

Hearing his animated description of this experience, I felt that I had really missed a golden opportunity. But as luck would have it, when I reached Korea in March after the Winter Olympics, Helena asked me to go with her to Pyeongchang for the Paralympics. I was thrilled! I was, as usual, fully covered with layers of woollens while my friend just wore a smart warm jacket. For Koreans, March is the end of winter, with temperatures exceeding 4 degrees Celsius. It was a nice two-hour drive in Helena's car and a unique experience for me to see her egg art work on display at the Paralympics venue. Being involved in the field of disability, I was moved by the performances of the athletes.

While I was comfortable in Mumbai during winter, Vasudev would come to India in the last week of December and sometimes again in February during the Lunar New Year holidays.

Experiencing the four seasons in Korea with all the travel, shopping and eating would not have been possible without the help of our smiling driver Jay. He was truly our Mr Dependable. His Korean name was Chung Joong-ho, but to keep it simple, he told us on the first day, 'Call me Jay'. He was a graduate from a university in California, US, where his parents and brothers lived. He was not happy in the US and felt some sort of discrimination there, so he decided to return to Korea and surrender his US passport. I remember when I first asked him, 'Why did you take up the job of a driver?' he said, 'Why not? I enjoy driving and I have been assigned to you because I know English.' I realized that no job is big or small, and that there is dignity of labour, especially in developed countries. Jay helped us settle in a new country, accompanied us for shopping that would have been very difficult without knowing the language, introduced us to the Korean cuisine and drove us around Korea to many interesting places, making our stint in Korea comfortable and enjoyable. 'How is Jay?' ask our friends who visited us in Korea and were shown around by him. He had become a part of our family.

Afterword

Korea has come a long way since when it was a country poorer than India in the 1960s. It is a well-developed, modern, vibrant democracy today. Being an Asian country, we in India can relate to the story of Korea's growth and development. Today, Korea's per capita income is nearly six times that of India's in terms of purchasing power parity. Their modern, world-class infrastructure with high-speed Internet, clean and hygienic facilities, and Hallyu entertainment stand out as hallmarks of an affluent society. Affluence brings confidence. It also poses a challenge to tradition. We could see a focussed effort on the part of the Korean government and administration to remind its citizens, especially the younger generations, of the nation's tradition and customs.

Young Koreans make an extra effort to learn English, and yet, almost all Koreans speak only their native language even if they know English. In contrast, Indians like to speak in English with their fellow Indians, at times necessitated by the absence of a common language. Libraries are full of books in Korean; international bestsellers are translated into Korean, which make them accessible to all. What we realized through Korea was that a country can develop and be an export powerhouse even if its people do not speak English. Same is the case with so many non-English-speaking countries in Europe and elsewhere.

The younger generations in Korea have realized the importance of knowing English in an integrated world, and we came across quite a few youngsters who have been to English-speaking countries just to brush up their English-speaking skills. A secretary in our company quit her job to go to the Philippines to improve her English. What we find interesting is that many Koreans who go abroad to study return to Korea thinking their country is much better and safer, which is probably true.

We saw many Korean parents take their young children to parks, beaches or mountains on weekends, where invariably there would be traditional displays. The most common sight is of the thatched-roof hanoks, a reminder of how earlier generations lived, and there are homestays to give that experience not just to foreigners but also to locals. In some of the parks we visited, there were houses displaying vintage kitchenware, telephones and furniture. There were also museums with ancient musical instruments. The entrance to the Gyeongbokgung Palace was free if one wore the traditional dress (hanbok).

Chuseok, a harvest festival, signals the onset of autumn. At this time, most Koreans visit their hometown to pay their respects to the spirits of their ancestors and offer them traditional food such as 'songpyeon'. Many of our friends would tell us how important it was to go to their ancestral homes and perform their duties. We realized then how tradition is carried forward despite modern development.

Despite their growth and prosperity, Koreans have their own set of challenges. People seemed to be always under some pressure. Gen Z shies from marriage or marries very late. Housing and education are expensive. Girls want more independence and a meaningful career, which the male-dominated society is still trying to grapple with.

On the one hand, there is a very low fertility rate, on the other, an aged population. Almost 20 per cent of the population is above the age of 65. The government is trying various ways to encourage people to have more kids. Speed dating events are organized with government support to encourage people to get married. Gender and income inequality still persist. Han Kang, who won the Nobel Prize for Literature in 2024, has highlighted gender inequality in Korea in her writings. *Parasite*, the movie that won multiple Academy Awards in 2020, brought out the issues of income inequality in a dramatic fashion.

Perception of India

While those Koreans who are well-travelled and well-read might have some knowledge about India, many don't. One may ask, why would they know about India? After all, before coming to Korea, what did we know about that country? We found that for almost everything, especially at SsangYong, Koreans shared a benchmark with Japan, the US and Germany. Nothing but the best! For them, quality was foremost, cost was secondary. They were always wary of quality if the goods came from China or India.

When we browsed through English newspapers in Korea, there would hardly be any article about India, and more often than not, when India was covered it was shown in poor light. So, it was no surprise to be asked things such as, 'Is India very poor?', 'Is corruption rampant?', 'How is the caste system?', 'Are people very religious?', 'How come people seem to be happy and celebrate festivals despite being poor?', 'Is India a safe country to visit?' and 'Why do you Indians take so much time to decide and act?' In India, we had not given much thought to these questions, but in Korea we had to respond as responsible Indian citizens. We tried to give a balanced view rather than paint either a rosy or a dark picture. The one positive thing we heard was the perception that Indians were good at mathematics and IT. Additionally, yoga was becoming popular thanks to awareness spread through International Yoga Day.

Our Korean boss had this interesting observation about us Indians, based on his interactions with the Mahindra & Mahindra employees in Korea. He would ask, 'Why do you guys move your head sometimes up and down, sometimes sideways? Why do you simply not say yes or no?' We were so used to nodding and shaking our heads that it had never occurred to us that someone would have difficulty in understanding the gesture or find it strange.

Our friends were all eager to visit India, but their first question would be, 'Is India a safe country to visit?' Then someone would cite an example of a thing experienced by somebody they knew and conclude that India is not safe and that people are not reliable. We would give them confidence that millions of people do travel all over India, and some stray cases should not deter them from visiting the country. The only word of caution was not to travel alone as a woman, and to preferably go in a group and rely on a reputed travel agency. We hope we do not have to say this in the near future.

We realized that when we are outside India, all of us have to be ambassadors of our country and put our best foot forward. People tend to generalize and form opinions. We kept reminding Koreans that India is a vast country where each state is like a country with its own language, customs and food, and hence they should not judge India or Indians based on their own experiences with a few. One learning we had was that as Indians, we should project our country in positive light wherever we are, especially in front of foreigners. Koreans would argue among themselves but rarely did we see them talk negatively about their own country or countrymen in front of foreigners.

When a Korean friend, Park Jong-baek, a lawyer, went to India for the first time and met us on his return, he told us, 'I saw two Indias in the last few days. One modern and the other a hundred years old.' That summed it up well.

Learnings for India and Indians

There is much to learn from the Korean growth story and the attitude of the Koreans.

We have seen the focus on infrastructure in India in the last few decades. We still have a long way to go but are happy to see modern infrastructure and technology development in India happening at a fast pace, with many of them of high global standards. We can now be proud to have so many new airports, ports, highways, bridges and tunnels all using the latest technology. All the good work on infrastructure will be futile if people do not follow discipline and ensure cleanliness.

In Korea, when they plan to develop an area, it is not just apartments to live in that is their concern but also schools, hospitals, parks, shopping complexes and, most importantly, bus and metro connectivity that are put in place simultaneously. Seoul and many big cities of the world have airports far from the city centre but with good bus and train connectivity.

One can feel quite safe with the traffic discipline in Korea. There are wide roads with well-marked lanes, pavements, no honking, driving and crossing discipline, and cameras everywhere to deter or check bad road behaviour. When we came back to India, we realized what foreigners from developed countries must experience when driving in or crossing a road in India. It took us a while to get used to the routine in India after over six years away. Initially, we kept 8 ft distance between two vehicles, only to find two and three wheelers squeezing in. Walking on the pavements or crossing the roads continues to be a daily challenge in India.

In 2023, our Korean friend came to Mumbai with her family. We went to their hotel to pick them up for dinner. As we got into our vehicle, our friend was surprised at not seeing a driver and congratulated us, as we were to drive them around in challenging traffic conditions.

In Korea, many presidents and senior political leaders have been sent to prison after their term. Some say it may be political vendetta. But leaders are held accountable. Even corporate founders or CEOs have been imprisoned. Nobody is above the law. That is the sign of an evolved, developed society. Citizens and activist groups hold silent protests on various issues, and it is a common sight on any weekend to see protestors near the City Hall or the Blue House in Seoul.

When we speak to our friends in India about Korea's discipline and hygiene, the first reaction from many of our friends is: 'It is a small country with fewer people.' We have to clarify to them that the density of population in Seoul is as high as that of, say, Chennai in India. It is not a question of fewer people but that of discipline. Korea is a small, homogeneous country, no doubt, but then what is stopping an Indian state to take the lead for others to emulate?

On our recent visit to Madhya Pradesh in 2024, we saw a ray of hope. Indore, which boasts of being the cleanest city in India for the last six years, is setting a good example for others to follow. What impressed us was the ownership and pride shown by the citizens to maintain cleanliness.

One thing we liked in the Korean administration was the role of the mayor of Seoul. He was like the CEO of the city and was fully responsible for the city's infrastructure. Big cities such as Seoul, London and New York have effective, empowered mayors. In India, the mayor does not have much say. In cities like Mumbai, we have seen lack of coordination across different departments hampering the city's growth and planned development.

A big takeaway for us was Korean's 'Uri Nara' or 'country first' attitude. It makes things so much easier if everyone thinks of the country first. Perhaps, the military training for boys helps. This attitude takes decades to be imbibed. One example of the commitment of the Koreans to a common cause comes to mind.

Once, our friends from India had come to Seoul to visit us. At that time, there was a political issue going on between Japan and Korea. There were calls to boycott Japanese goods to teach the country a lesson. Most of the Koreans boycotted, so much so that some of the Japanese shops like Uniqlo offered discounts of over 80 per cent to clear their stocks. Our friends visiting us from India had a field day shopping in the absence of Korean customers. As they came out after shopping, with bags in both hands, our driver asked in a hurt voice, 'You are buying Japanese goods? We are boycotting them.'

Tourism in Korea has got a boost thanks to the soft power generated by the K-wave. People want to visit Korea after listening to K-pop, watching K-dramas and tasting K-cuisine. Our own Bollywood, which has been popular with the Indian diaspora around the world, can take a cue from Koreans and make Indian films more popular with the international audience.

When we went to Seoul in 2023, we met quite a few young Indian families visiting on their own, all having been influenced after watching K-dramas. So long as it is just tourism, it is fine. But we get calls from many anxious parents saying that their son or daughter wants to go to Korea to study or make a career. We make it clear to them that they will have to learn the language and that getting a job will not be easy, since there are not too many new jobs available and first priority will always be given to Koreans. Even if one gets a job, rising up the corporate ladder will be another challenge. Our advice to these youngsters enamoured by the K-wave is that please do not drown in the K-wave. Navigate your way through this K-culture tsunami and nurture our own rich Indian cultural heritage.

Personally, we learnt a lot in Korea. We are now perhaps as paranoid about punctuality and cleanliness as the Koreans, which makes adjustment difficult in India. Our health improved with timely dinners and regular evening walks in Korea, which we still continue to do in India. We were fortunate to make many friends from different countries, which helped us to learn more about the other countries.

As our term in Korea was coming to an end, some friends asked us, 'Why don't you settle in Korea? Sudha knows the language and you have so many friends.' Of course, it was easier said than done. We had no plans to stay back in Korea, keeping with our son's theory of circular migration in his book *India Moving: A History of Migration*, where he describes how most Indian migrants who go out for work tend to return to their roots!

We were fortunate to return to India on 31 December 2019, after enjoying the warmth of our Korean friends in the winter, with farewell parties almost every day in December. We did not know then that a pandemic (till then not in our vocabulary) was lurking round the corner, which would have spoilt our party if we were to return in March 2020 as per our original plan. During the Covid-19 lockdown, when house help was not available, our experience of living without house help in Korea came to our aid. While eating Indian mangoes on our return, we realized how much we had missed them in the last six summers. K-dramas on Netflix, during the lockdown, helped us to stay connected with Korea in some way and also helped us remember the good times we had there. We remember it fondly even now.

We must remember that even Korean society was once like ours. They have evolved over the years to reach where they are today. We can take some learnings from the Korean growth story. The way people in India, including hawkers and street vendors, have embraced digital payments, especially after the pandemic, and the number of start-ups springing up gives us hope that technology can be a game changer.

As Dr Pawan Goenka, former managing director of Mahindra & Mahindra and chairman of Ssangyong used to say, 'If we can combine Korea's execution excellence and process-discipline with India's adaptability and frugality, we can truly be world class.'

Acknowledgements

We thank friends and family members who suggested that we document our experiences in Korea, in English whenever we narrated some incidents about the country.

We are grateful to all our Korean friends who gave us a great experience of living in Korea, and to our colleagues in Mahindra & Mahindra who gave us the opportunity to work in Korea.

We are indebted to Bharat Doshi, our family friend and mentor, for motivating us to write the book and for his valuable inputs after going through the draft manuscript.

We are grateful to Sanjeev Saksena, from SsangYong and Mahindra, who patiently went through the manuscript and gave useful suggestions.

Many thanks to Prof. Dae Ryun Chang for sharing insights about the success of the Korean wave and for clearing our doubts from time to time.

We are thankful to our friend and colleague from SsangYong, Lee Soo-won, for his useful inputs, and his enthusiastic and prompt responses to all our queries.

Our friends Shashi Maudgal and Sachin Satpute, who have worked in Korea as CEOs, shared some anecdotes; we are obliged to them for it.

It was a delight to work with our editor Swati Chopra and her team at Juggernaut comprising Wesley D'Souza, Nishtha Kapil and Smita Mathur, who were very professional and refined our writing beautifully. Kudos to Gunjan Ahlawat who designed the cover, and Silvan Borer who made the illustration for the cover.

The book benefitted from the critical inputs received from our daughter-in-law Divya Ravindranath who painstakingly went through the manuscript and improved the language.

We had the 'home' advantage of having a writer in the family. Our author son Chinmay Tumbe's inputs and guidance helped a lot. Our grandson Siddhartha, who has often seen his father busy writing, was surprised to see even his grandparents engaged in writing a book and asked us, 'You too?' We said, 'Yes, we two!'

A Note on the Authors

Sudha and **Vasudev** first met in a local train in Mumbai while going to their respective offices. Their journey continues, both being travel lovers, albeit to other countries. They have been married for 40 years and celebrated their thirtieth to thirty-fifth wedding anniversaries in South Korea.

Sudha Huzurbazar Tumbe is a Marathi writer, teacher and counsellor. She is the author of *Saptarangi Korea: Ek Anubhav*, published by Granthali in 2022, and *Rang Jeevanche* (2025). She is a polyglot, fluent in six languages, including Korean. An avid reader, she is now a Marathi writer on topics that are regularly published in various Marathi magazines.

She has been associated with various institutions as a teacher or counsellor in Mumbai, such as VJTI, SNDT, National Association for Blind, Lotus Eye Hospital and College of Optometry. She has recently conceptualized a disability awareness programme in Marathi on Granthali

Pratibhangan's YouTube channel, interviewing experts on different disabilities in India. In South Korea, Sudha volunteered for the Seoul Namdaemun Police, Anna's House and Korea Dyslexia Association, and was appointed as the Gangnam publicity ambassador.

Vasudev Tumbe joined Mahindra & Mahindra, Mumbai, in 1982 as a professional cricketer to represent their team in various cricket tournaments – having represented and captained Mumbai and West Zone Under-22 and university cricket teams. Being a qualified cost accountant, after his cricket-playing days, he worked in various roles in finance, accounts and costing, and was vice president (finance & accounts, automotive division) from 2008 to 2013 before going to South Korea.

From July 2013 to December 2019, he was the vice president and CFO of SsangYong Motor Company, South Korea, a listed USD 3 billion subsidiary of Mahindra & Mahindra. He also served on the board of the Indian Chamber of Commerce in Korea (ICCK) from 2013 to 2019 and was its chairman from August 2017 to December 2019, closely working with the Indian embassy in South Korea to promote India–Korea trade and investment.

Glossary of Korean Words in the Book

Korean words in English	Meaning	Korean script
Ahjussi	Elderly man	아저씨
Ajumma	Elderly woman	아줌마
Aneyo	No	아니요
Annyeonghaseyo	Hello (greeting)	안녕하세요
Appa	Father	아빠
Baeg-iljanchi	Hundredth day after birth celebration	백일잔치
Banchan	Side dishes	반찬
Beojkkoch	Cherry blossom	벚꽃
Bibimbap	Rice with vegetables or meat mixed with gochujang paste	비빔밥
Bujang	General Manager	부장
Buk	North	북

Korean words in English	Meaning	Korean script
Bulgogi	Grilled beef	불고기
Busajang	Vice president	부사장
Chaebol	A large, family-owned business conglomerate	재벌
Chajang	Deputy general manager	차장
Chi-maek	Short for chicken and beer	치맥
Chingu	Friend	친구
Chuseok	Harvest festival	추석
Dabang	Cafe	다방
Daehan Minguk	Republic of Korea	대한민국
Dak-galbi	A type of chicken barbeque	닭갈비
Danpung	Fall colours	단풍
Doljanchi	First birthday celebration	돌잔치
Eobseoyo	Don't have	없어요
Eog	Hundred million	억
Eolmaeyo	How much?	얼마예요
Eomma	Mother	엄마
Gamsahamnida	Thank you	감사합니다
Gani, Kani, Rogi, Tayo	Names of buses based on colours	카니, 라니, 로기, 타요

Glossary of Korean Words in the Book

Korean words in English	Meaning	Korean script
Geonbae	Cheers	건배
Gochujang	Spicy red pepper paste	고추장
Gunbam	Roasted chestnut	군밤
Gungoguma	Roasted sweet potato	군고구마
Gwajang	Manager	과장
Haemol pajeon	Seafood pancake	해물파전
Haenyo	Women divers	해녀
Hagwon	Coaching classes	학원
Hallyu	Korean wave	한류
Hana, Dul, Set	One, two, three	하나, 둘, 셋
Hanbok	Traditional Korean dress	한복
Hangang	Han River	한강
Hangug-Saram	Korean person	한국사람
Hangul	Korean alphabets	한글
Hanok	Traditional thatched-roof or tiled-roof house	한옥
Hwajangsil	Toilet	화장실
Hwangabjanchi	Sixtieth birthday celebration	환갑잔치
Imo	Aunty	이모
Insa	Bow	인사
Jagae	Mother-of-pearls	자개

Korean words in English	Meaning	Korean script
Japchae	Glass noodles stir-fried	잡채
Jeonse	An arrangement where the payable amount is only deposit, no rent	전세
Jimjilbang	Public bath	찜질방
Keranpang	Egg bread	계란빵
Kimbap	Rice and vegetables or meat rolled in seaweed	김밥
Kimchi	Salted and fermented cabbage	김치
Kkakajusaeyo	Discount please/cut the price	깍아주세요
Maekju	Beer	맥주
Makgeolli	Rice wine	막걸리
Mann	Ten thousand	만
Minhwa	A traditional painting style	민화
Myolchi	Anchovy	멸치
Nam	South	남
Nampyeon	Husband	남편
Ne	Yes	네
Noraebang	Karaoke bar	노래방
Eomug	Fish cake	어묵

Glossary of Korean Words in the Book

Korean words in English	Meaning	Korean script
Oegug-Saram	Foreigner	외국 사람
Ondol	Traditional heating system	온돌
Palli Palli	Quick	빨리 빨리
Sajang	President	사장
Samgyetang	A type of chicken soup	삼계탕
San	Mountain	산
Sangmu	Director	상무
Seollal	Lunar new year	설날
So-maek	Short for soju and beer	소맥
Soju	Local alcohol made from rice or barley	소주
Songpyeon	Rice cake for Chuseok	송편
Tteok	A sweet rice cake	떡
Tteokbokki	Spicy rice cake	떡볶이
Unni	Sister	언니
Uri Nara	Our country	우리 나라
Yogiyo	Hey there/ listen, calling out	요기요